GOD
and
COUNTRY

TOMMY NELSON

GOD
and
COUNTRY

What the Bible Says
About How Christians Should
Relate to Government

FIDELIS
PUBLISHING

FIDELIS PUBLISHING ®

ISBN: 9781956454284
ISBN (eBook): 9781956454291

God and Country
What the Bible Says about How Christians Should Relate to Government

Cover Design by Diana Lawrence
Interior Design by LParnell Book Services
Edited by Amanda Varian

Order at www.faithfultext.com for a significant discount. Email info@ fidelispublishing.com to inquire about bulk purchase discounts.

Fidelis Publishing, LLC Winchester, VA • Nashville, TN
www.fidelispublishing.com

Manufactured in the United States of America

10 9 8 7 6 5 4 3 2 1

FIDELIS
PUBLISHING

Contents

Editor's Note

Fidelis Publishing is honored to bring you this book from a pastor I have known for decades. In a world awash with lies, chaos, and confusion, Tommy Nelson is a calm yet passionate voice for the gospel. His expositional teaching through the Bible is unmatched for sound theology, clarity, and even entertainment in my forty-plus years in the Church.

The book you're about to read comes from the transcription of the eight-part series delivered to Denton Bible Church. Thorough editing has been done, but we decided to preserve as much of the feel of listening to a sermon as we could. I ask you to let the words hit your mind the way they do as you sit in the pew with a congregation around you and your Bible in your lap.

If you'd like to listen to the original sermons, go to: https://dentonbible.org/media/media-library/view-series/god-and-country/. There you'll find a treasure trove of wisdom and discipleship through years of consistent ministry of the Word.

Grace and peace,
Gary Terashita
Fidelis Publishing

1
God and the Politicians

PSALM 82
A PSALM OF ASAPH

God takes His position in His assembly;
He judges in the midst of the gods.
How long will you judge unjustly
And show partiality to the wicked? Selah
Vindicate the weak and fatherless;
Do justice to the afflicted and destitute.
Rescue the weak and needy;
Save them from the hand of the wicked.
They do not know nor do they understand;
They walk around in darkness;
All the foundations of the earth are shaken.
I said, "You are gods,
And all of you are sons of the Most High.
Nevertheless you will die like men,
And fall like one of the princes."
Arise, God, judge the earth!
For you possess all the nations.

I'm going to start this book with a look at Psalm 82. You'll find the psalm is self-interpretive. God rules man through the institutions of the home, the government, and the church. This opening chapter looks at the second aspect: God and government. Let's consider what we will call God and country or how God deals with the nations. He is the God of the heavens and the earth. He is the God of nations. All things continue beneath God's sovereign authority.

Augustine took thirteen years to write his book *The City of God* from AD 413 to 426. He wrote it because, at that time, the Roman Empire was imploding in its own immorality and the German tribesmen were about to take it over. The charge was made that the reason the empire fell was because Christianity angered the gods of Rome. Augustine's response was, "We're not the cause for your problem. The cause for your problem is we weren't *the solution*." He stated that, in the City of Man, man is the ultimate ruler for his own glorification, including the lust of the flesh, lust of the eyes, and the pride of life. The lust of the flesh is called hedonism. The lust of the eyes is called materialism. The pride of life is called humanism. Augustine wrote that the City of Man passes away. He believed the Church is the City of God. We're a people who have foundations rooted in the heavens and we are going to be here long after all others are gone. That became his classic, *The City of God*, about how a believer in Jesus Christ lives in a world that is failing, dying, and passing away.

We Christians are strangers and aliens. We are in the world but we're not of the world. We're a blessing to this world but this is not our home. We have no human king. We have a heavenly King and our longing is for our Father who art in heaven—for His kingdom to come, and His will to be done on earth as it is in heaven.

That is of what Psalm 82 speaks. In verse 1, the author gives you God's position in the nation of Israel.

God takes His position in His assembly;
He judges in the midst of the gods [rulers].

God takes His stand in His own congregation. He judges in the midst of the gods. God stands in their midst, whistles, and calls all the politicians to His feet.

"Rulers" is translated "gods" here because that is what a politician is. God has bestowed upon him freedom to judge. Can a ruler bring death upon whom he is pleased? Yes, he can. Can he bring life and clemency? Yes, he can. If you recall God's authority He gave to Nebuchadnezzar: ". . . all the peoples, nations and men of every language feared and trembled before him; whomever he wished he killed and whomever he wished he spared alive; and whomever he wished he elevated and whomever he wished he humbled" (Daniel 5:19).

Now, of course, God is absolutely in control, but relatively speaking, God can and does bestow power and authority where He pleases. He gives authority to men. They are called "gods," but God takes His stand as sovereign. He is central. He is the one man must look to.

I prayed once in the House of Representatives in Washington, and on the face of the balcony, there is a series of representations of leaders of government and law. Some politicians, some philosophers, some popes. Do you know who is right in the middle? Moses. Looking right at you. I got ready to pray and I looked up and there was the representative of the Law of God looking at me, overseeing what takes place. It was a humbling moment. That's what He does to the rulers; God takes His stand. He is the one who must be central because without God, man has no standard of right and wrong by which to rule.

All may have personal opinions of what gives pragmatically the most pleasing results at the time, but we can have no final standard of what is right or wrong without the infinite personal God of the Bible. Also, in the House of Representatives, if you look *behind* you, do you know what's on the wall? "In God We Trust." As a matter of fact, the most spiritual place I have ever spoken at is our nation's capital.

The only places that rival it are West Point and Annapolis because when you have government and when you have the military, you'd better have "God with us." There are no atheists in foxholes. That is God's position in His own congregation. Israel's greatest possession as a nation was God. In a sense, that was Israel's boast. Don't come to see the mountains, don't come to see the rivers, don't come to see the streams, don't come to see the shoreline, come and see God.

The apostle Paul said, "Then what advantage has the Jew? Great in every respect. First of all, they were entrusted with the oracles of God" (Romans 3:1). Israel had a Bible. There was a land of Canaan, and in that, you had twelves tribes. One tribe was called Benjamin, with one city in it called Jerusalem. In Jerusalem, there was a temple. In that temple, there was the Holy of Holies. In that Holy of Holies, was an acacia wood box. In that box, you had not gold or silver, but stone—the cheapest material you can possess. And yet it is the most precious artifact in the universe. What is written on that stone is the Law of God, the Ten Commandments engraved by the finger of God.

The Holy of Holies, the temple, Jerusalem, Benjamin, and Israel, and the strength of the nation is in a small place—the Word of God. Plato said as one goes through life, one must find "the best opinions of men and hold them as to a boat in a storm unless one has a more certain word of God." If only the word could become flesh, we would have the final political system, the final philosophy, and the final religion.

Because if God becomes a man as your prophet, priest, and king, you have settled the issue of philosophy, religion, and government. You are now the most blessed of nations. Should you forget and rebel, in that day, "you will surely die" (Genesis 2:17). And so God takes His seat in His nation.

In verse 2, you see God's problem: politicians who can be bought.

How long will you judge unjustly
And show partiality to the wicked? Selah

Rulers who are no longer seeking the will of God become career politicians. They simply want to be elected. "How long will you judge unjustly and show partiality to the wicked?"—so it is when justice is for sale. Whenever a Jew became king, he had to be anointed by God. Then he had to make his own copy of the Old Testament law, which is probably Deuteronomy 27 and 28, the blessings and cursings. He had to copy it in the presence of a Levitical priest so he couldn't change any part of it. Then he had to "read it all the days of his life" (Deuteronomy 17:19).

A king was the only man in the Old Testament commanded to read his Bible. "That his heart may not be lifted up above his countrymen" (Deuteronomy 17:20). He couldn't become arrogant because he stood continually before God. When he was sworn in, he stood by a pillar called *Yakiyn* or *Jachin*, which means "God establishes."

He took an oath before God to follow God and the people to follow him. *That* is how a king becomes a king. Because in political science, it doesn't matter about the governing system you have. The wild card is who governs those who govern. Who rules the ruler or the monarch or the democracy or the elected officials or the Republican representative government. It doesn't matter which system one has. There's nothing magic about any form of government. The question is "Who rules those who rule?" The man or woman I vote for, all I ask is for him or her to fear the living God.

That's why in American history there are two professions who wear black robes because they're meant to disappear. You are not to see them as individuals. It's as if they are holy and separated from earth. One is a pastor. He is supposed to disappear. He is eyes and ears and a voice. He can't be influenced. He is to faithfully explain the Word of God. The other profession is that of a judge. He must be eyes and ears and a gavel. He cannot be bought.

In Chicago in the 1920s, a fellow took over the city because he made so much money during prohibition, running moonshine, he could buy the police and politicians.

Al Capone owned the government and Chicago had to form a special force with an agent named Elliot Ness. The group he assembled was called "The Untouchables" because you couldn't bribe them. That's what a politician must be. He must be the untouchable who seeks the will of God.

Can corruption ever happen? Do you remember a ruler named Pontius Pilate who found Jesus innocent six times? Yet someone said, "If you free this man, you are no longer a friend of Caesar." Pilate had to make a choice between sending an innocent man to his death or his career, and he sent the man to his death. He tried to get away from it by washing his hands. Even the Roman solders who guarded the tomb took money to say Christ did not rise from the dead. Rulers have always been easily bought. It was not to be so in Israel.

Can politicians get corrupted? Always have. Always will. Alexis de Tocqueville was a French nobleman, aristocrat, politician, writer, and author. He visited to appraise this new upstart place called the United States, and he noticed in the places he went there were churches, Protestant churches preaching the Bible. He said, "America is great because America is good. When America is no longer good, America will no longer be great."

God's *purpose* for a politician is in verses 3 and 4.

Vindicate the weak and fatherless;
Do justice to the afflicted and destitute.
Rescue the weak and needy;
Save them from the hand of the wicked.

It's what a ruler is supposed to do. He is to vindicate the weak, the orphan, and the fatherless. To do justice to the afflicted and the destitute.

Politicians are meant to be selfless servants who are above history and personal desires. They are to stand and deliver man from the jungle. Because when you can be bought, you are now in Chicago 1920. All law is gone. Welcome to the jungle.

The purpose of government is found in 1 Peter 2:14, "For the punishment of evildoers and the praise of those who do right." That's the purpose of a politician. They are the plumbline of God's law. Romans 13:4 says they do "not bear the sword for nothing, but they are ministers of God, who bring wrath on the one who preaches evil." Paul continues, "For because of this you also pay taxes, because rulers are servants of God, devoting themselves to this very thing" (author's paraphrase). Paul likens our taxes to a tithe because rulers are servants of God. When someone gets kidnapped, we don't have to go organize a mob and hang him.

We pay people to inflict justice. They're called politicians and police and we pay them as we would preachers and priests. In the same way we pay the military. That's why in the New Testament, you have two professions who are honored. Four fishermen (who became four apostles) and four centurions. Church and state. What do you need to have order? You need a state with authority and the church to inform them. The church to teach the law and the state to protect it. They are the two edges of the sword. A king and a priest. Whenever you lose that sword, you are in the jungle.

This is God's purpose for a politician. To take care of the weak. Back to Psalm 82, verse 5:

> *They do not know nor do they understand;*
> *They walk around in darkness;*
> *All the foundations of the earth are shaken.*

Here is a politician's *demise.* This is when a country enters the Dark Ages. "They," meaning the politicians, "do not know nor do they understand. They walk in darkness." They don't understand what? They don't understand the authority of God and the purpose of a ruler. As a result, they walk in darkness, "and all the foundations are shaken." Down falls civilization.

When the Puritans came to the New World, they started with about 100 people there on the *Mayflower.* Eventually, 30,000 Puritans came from England after its ruler was changed. It was called the Puritan exodus. They all came over and settled on the East Coast. They instituted "The Old Deluder Satan Act," which said if you had a town of fifty people, you had to have a school because they recognized if they were going to have a representative government where the people put up the leaders, you had to have an educated people who could read their Bibles. "For the entrance of thy word giveth light." The Puritans started a college—Harvard—for the training of men who would be their congregational ministers. Because you can't have a civilization without God.

When those who settled built a city, they put in a courthouse and then a church. It was again both edges of the sword. That was the foundation of our New England, Ivy League colleges. Only Cornell was not begun by Christians for the purpose of Christian education. Dartmouth? It was the legacy of Moor's Indian Training School founded by Reverend Eleazar Wheelock in 1754 to educate Native American converts after the first Great Awakening. Horace Greeley said, "It is impossible to enslave, mentally or socially, a Bible-reading people. The principles of the Bible are the groundwork of human freedom."

Communism is an attempt of rule without God. It is atheistic—Russia being the classic example. You know what always follows an atheist revolution? Book burning. You cannot have people thinking independently. You have to remove their literature so you can take their minds captive. Not to be ugly, but if you go to South America and in strong Catholic countries, the Bible has been on the index of forbidden books. If I'm a priest, I don't want you thinking for yourself. "You will do what I tell you to and keep you in the system." That is why the blessed idea of the Protestant movement is the priesthood of the believer. We can all know personally the Word of God. You couldn't have had American education without American Protestantism.

Francis Schaeffer said, unless there is an absolute to judge society, society is absolute.

In 1845, Karl Marx said, "Religion is the opiate of the people." Sigmund Freud said, "The psychoanalysis of individual human beings, however, teaches us with quite special insistence that the god of each of them is formed in the likeness of his father, that his personal relation to God depends on his relation to his father in the flesh and oscillates and changes along with that relation, and that at bottom God is nothing other than an exalted father."[1] Friedrich Nietzsche said, "The belief in authority is the source of conscience; which is therefore not the voice of God in the heart of man, but the voice of some men in man."[2] Philosopher Jean-Paul Sartre said, "No finite point has meaning without an infinite reference point." You can't speak about man, government, love, sex, whatever, without an infinite reference point to define them.

Now, these men I just read to you are politicians, scientists, psychologists, philosophers. They all contributed to the twentieth century. They were all atheists and they produced the century of blood. You cannot have civilization without Yahweh, the infinite personal God of the heaven and the earth, the sea and the dry land, of which man is created uniquely in the image of God. There must be a final standard for right and wrong. God makes Himself known indeed.

If I were God, and I was going to start a nation to preserve us from what was going to come in the Enlightenment, I would take the best of the Reformation and I would land them on a shore. I would start a nation around them before they got educated beyond their intelligence and got rid of God.

On the next page, the painting in the United Nations was painted in 1904 by Paul Robert and titled *Justice Lifts the Nations*. Down at the bottom of the painting there are two lawyers. They're arguing over a document. Both of the lawyers have families behind them.

To the right above them, there's a man with a gold shield on his chest: that's the sergeant at arms and he's got a sword. He's going to enforce the ruling. Above him, you see the judges who are listening but their eyes are not on the lawyers. Their eyes are lifted to the glowing lady. She's the personification of justice. Those judges are looking to the lady of light.

She is justice. She has scales in her hands. She can't be deceived. She's looking away from the people. She can't be bought. She's holding a sword in her left hand because she is life or death, and that sword is resting on something. What is it? It's the Bible.

There's a famous book written during the Reformation by Samuel Rutherford, a Scottish Presbyterian minister, called *Lex Rex*. *Lex rex* is Latin—meaning, "the law is king." Not the king is law. But the law is king. That's why our country has survived thus far. We have an echo of Sinai in our Constitution of the Judeo-Christian idea of right and wrong. Society's doom is found in Psalm 82:5.

They do not know nor do they understand;
They walk around in darkness;
All the foundations of the earth are shaken.

Whenever you corrupt leadership, that nation is in jeopardy. Being Satan is not difficult. You must reach the governors. You must reach the politicians. You must reach the theologians, the educators, the philosophers, and the parents. Then you have the nation.

In verse 5b, as a result, "All the foundations"—meaning the rulers, who make our laws—"of the earth are shaken." When you have darkened politicians, you have career men and women succeeding in their ambitions. What you have then is a tsunami. The earth is moved. In 1906 in San Francisco, everything came down because the earth moved. This is what happens when godless people are placed in authority.

There are nine on the Supreme Court so you can't ever have a tie. Whenever the Supreme Court says it's wrong to pray in school, no more prayer. And so it is. It's interesting, you can trace America's demise from that moment. You can start there. As a matter of fact, you can trace the demise of America by the *nature* of the forbidden prayer. We prayed for our leaders, our parents, our teachers, and our students. It's as if God took us at our word and said, "I'm out of it." The foundations were destroyed.

How do you judge a rebellious teenager? Give him freedom. Give him over to himself. That's what God did. He dealt with us like a rebellious eighteen-year-old. The Supreme Court says no prayer. So, no prayer. Then in 1973, the miracle of the womb is declared not a human. Sixty million and counting have died. Then later on the historic family—father, mother, child—is not a family. Sodomites are now included. Soon after you see rainbow lights covering the White House. That's a scary feeling. I said to my wife, "I have lived too long."

When Beto O'Rourke was asked, "Do you think religious institutions like colleges, churches, charities should lose their tax-exempt status if they oppose same-sex marriage?" O'Rourke replied, "Yes."[3] This from a man who wanted to be president. "The foundations are shaken."

Verses 6 and 7 are sobering ideas:

I said, "you are gods,
And all of you are sons of the Most High.
Nevertheless you will die like men,
And fall like one of the princes."

Though men be "gods," or designated regents ordained by God, they can fall like any "one of the princes." Just as God could remove a Pharaoh or Sennacherib of Assyria or Nebuchadnezzar, so He can remove any ruler of His covenant people. How easily can God remove any leader, and any country that rejects His sovereign will? World history is a testimony to the removal of any arrogant mouth of great boasts against God.

Assyria, Babylon, Persia, Greece, and Rome. All these empires that arose against God—they're gone. They're Nova specials. They're National Geographic hour-long specials filmed with a drone. They're archeological digs—they're gone. Jericho is the oldest city on earth. You can go down to nine civilizations digging down and find it's gone. In verse 8, here is God's solution, our only hope. God will arise.

Arise, God, judge the earth!
For you possess all the nations.

If you circle the word "arise," you can contrast it with verse 7: "you will fall." Arise, O God. There is a book in the Bible where you see the heavens rolled back and the King of Heaven asserting His rule upon the earth, judging the earth, and then possessing the nations. It's called the Second Coming. Jesus is in control. "Maranatha, Lord, come soon." We hasten the day of God.

In Romans 8:18–22, creation is pictured as longing for the coming of Christ to rid the world of all of the vermin who have done their worst.

Who are we? We're *Robin Hood*. In the classic story, the king is Richard. He has been usurped by evil King John, his wicked brother who has brought darkness to Nottingham. Robin of Locksley will not submit to evil. He fights and he struggles to bring the people out of darkness and unto himself. What kind of men does he have? Merry men. You're always happy when you're following the truth. Robin struggles and keeps struggling. Why does he keep struggling? Why does he never relent? He has hope. His hope? Richard is going to return. To Richard alone, he will bow. That's who the Christian is. We're Robin Hood. We're the merry men, and we fight against evil. And we will not bow the knee to evil. We will bow the knee to only one, and that is the appearing of our great King and not until then.

In the '60s, we had a lot of problems. My generation *said* we had a lot of problems. That's good to realize. My generation said we had to fix them. That's good too. But we didn't go back to the Bible's authority like Luther did in the Reformation. We just *kept on going.* We lost confidence in Christ. We tried drugs—it was a philosophic thing rather than recreational. We couldn't find truth in philosophy and human reason. We felt if we took a trip and had a cosmic consciousness, maybe then we could find truth. That was the purpose of drugs. It was to take you some place reason wouldn't go. What did we get out of it? Manson and Woodstock. The '60s didn't work.

So we went to Eastern religion. We abandoned anything Judeo-Christian and Western. It didn't work. We didn't go *back*—we went *on* and ended up in violence, addiction, illegitimacy, divorce, Watergate, overdoses, and venereal disease.

We're still not going back. We're still trying to go *on.* Now "Cultural Marxism" is the thought of the day. It's communism revamped. We're trying to find answers through atheism. Once again, we're trying to legislate atheism. No longer are the capitalists the bad guys but the white, heterosexual

Christians who are born of a certain gender. It's called systemic racism, cancel culture, and being "woke." We're the only people—followers of Christ—who have the sense to say, "We've got to go *back* to the Creator of the heavens and the earth, sea, and the dry land."

It was during the Protestant Reformation that the watchword became *Ad fonte*, meaning "back to the fountain"—the fountain being the authority of the Bible as the final word on truth. Back to that which had been the foundation of all true civilization and all true government. That which alone stood up to the claim—the Word of God.

2

Beautiful Savior— Lord of the Nations

Do you listen to the words to the songs on the radio? They're all about redemption. Lost loves, lost lives, lost dreams, lost cultures, and the pain they bring. Man knows something is broken but we just don't know how to fix it.

> *This is an evil in everything that is done under the sun, that there is one fate for everyone. Furthermore, the hearts of the sons of mankind are full of evil, and insanity is in their hearts throughout their lives. Afterward they go to the dead.* (Ecclesiastes 9:3)

The Gospel of Matthew is written to the Jews, which in and of itself would be an apologetic for the validity of Christ. Because what did Matthew do for a living? He was a tax collector—the public enemy of Israel. A tax collector bought the right from Rome to collect taxes. It was auctioned. The right to tax your own people. They would tax them a flat rate plus whatever they could extort. For a tax collector to write a book about the Messiah is like Paul, the enemy of the church, becoming its leading apostle. Paul's very identity was an apologetic for the faith. So with Matthew and his Gospel. Matthew's argument is twofold. To prove Jesus was the King of the Jews. And if He's the King, where is the kingdom?

The Bible says, in the kingdom the lion will lay down with the lamb, and so the natural response of the Jew would be, "If Christ is the king, then where is the kingdom?" Matthew's argument is going to answer that. It's in the term ORPA. The kingdom was *offered* in John the Baptist and Christ by His words and works and by the Twelve who went out preaching. The R is for *rejected*. Israel rejected Christ. They rejected the apostles. They put Him on the cross and then they persecuted His witnesses. The P is for *postponement*. The kingdom has now been given to others in a mystery form of the kingdom of God.

What's that group called in whom the kingdom now rests? The Church. He came to the remnant of Israel who believed and then to the Gentiles. O-R-P, offered, rejected, and postponed. Postponed because there *is* going to be a literal kingdom someday. Matthew 24 describes the Second Coming of Christ to rule. Offered, rejected, postponed, and then *appearing* (ORPA). That is Matthew's argument. The first four chapters of Matthew are called the *presentation* of the King. If you were going to convince a nation of Jews that Jesus was the King, how would you do it? Matthew looks at His genealogy. You trace Him back to David and to

Abraham. Then you would look at His virgin birth. Emmanuel, "God with us."

Then you would look at His worship by the wise men. "Where is He who has been born King of the Jews?" (Matthew 2:2). Then I would look at His Moses-like flight down to Egypt and then His return when the enemies were dead. Jesus is the final Mosaic prophet promised who will be the final word of God (Deuteronomy 18:15). Then I would look at His being from Nazareth, "He will be called a Nazarene" (Matthew 2:23). Then I would tell of John the Baptist, the forerunner. I would look at Jesus's baptism where God said, "This is My beloved Son" (Matthew 3:17). Then His temptation where Satan was defeated by Him. That is the first four chapters of Matthew, the presentation of the King.

Chapters 5, 6, and 7 are called the Sermon on the Mount. Here we go from the presentation of the King to the preaching of the King. "You've heard it was said . . . but I say to you." Jesus is the final arbiter of the word of God. "Do not presume that I came to abolish the Law or the Prophets . . . but to fulfill. Not the smallest letter or stroke of a letter shall pass from the Law, until all is accomplished!" (Matthew 5:17–18). That's the *preaching* of the King. Then in Matthew 8 and 9, we see the *power* of the King. Ten miracles over demons, disease, disability, death, and natural disaster. Christ dominates them by His mere words.

So we go from the presentation of the King to the preaching of the King to the power of the King. And these ten miracles are grouped in a deliberate way: three miracles and then a discourse; three miracles then a discourse; four miracles and then a discourse. The discourses are on the price demanded to follow Him because the doors are going to be shutting. Of these groupings, they all follow the same layout. He did a miracle over a Jew, then a miracle over a Gentile, and then He returned and did another miracle over a Jew. Then, after each, a discourse on the price demanded to follow Him. Such was the course of His ministry. Christ came to the Jew, turned to the Gentiles in the church, and then someday will return to Israel. In each phase, discipleship will be costly.

In the first triad of miracles, Jesus came to a leper, then a centurion, then Peter's mother-in-law. In the next grouping, He stilled the winds and waves over the twelve disciples who are Jewish. Then He went to the Gerasene demoniac who was a Gentile. Then He came back to the Jews. It goes Jew, Gentile, Jew, Jew, Gentile, Jew. Why did Matthew lay it out like that? Because Jesus's ministry followed this path.

As a matter of fact, in the last grouping, it went like this: There was a sick and dying Jewish girl whose father was the head of the synagogue, a man named Jairus. She's twelve. How many tribes are there in Israel? Twelve. Jesus went to heal the little Jewish girl of the synagogue. On the way there, He was detained by a Gentile woman. She had an issue of blood; she couldn't get into a synagogue. She spent everything she had on doctors and she was worse off than when she began, just like the Gentiles. Jesus was delayed going to the Jewish girl by healing the Gentile woman. She touched the hem of His garment because she knew as a Gentile she couldn't touch Him. She was probably thinking, *I'll touch His garment, no. The tassel, no. The hem of the tassel of the hem of His garment, and He'll never know.*

Jesus stopped. "Who touched My garments?" His disciples declared *everybody* was touching Him! Christ said in so many words, "Oh, no, I know the difference between a sightseer and a seeker." He made her give a witness to all the Jews as to what He could do for a Gentile (as the church does now). Then Jesus continued to the little Jewish girl in the synagogue, but now she wasn't sick—she was dead (so is Israel today). Everyone laughed at Him. Yet He brought her back from the dead. Does that sound familiar? Christ went to the twelve tribes, got detained by a Gentile who couldn't get in the synagogue, healed her and she gave a witness, then He went back to a little girl who's dead, and He raised her. Jew, Gentile, Jew.

Matthew is showing what is to be the ministry of Christ. He came to the Jew first, then also to the Greek, and then He will return to the Jew. Now that's just the hors d'oeuvre—you ought to see the main course here. In Matthew 8:23–27, there is the miracle on the sea over the Jewish disciples. In verse 28 there is another miracle when Jesus went to the "other side." Do you know what the other side is? It's the eastern side of the Sea of Galilee; it's the Gentile area. He performed a miracle over the classic picture of the pagan Gentile world. God and countries.

> *And when He came to the other side into the*
> *country of the Gadarenes, two demon-possessed*
> *men confronted Him as they were coming out*
> *of the tombs. They were so extremely violent*
> *that no one could pass by that way. And they*

cried out, saying, "What business do You have with us, Son of God? Have you come here to torment us before the time?" Now there was a herd of many pigs feeding at a distance from them. And the demons begged Him, saying, "If you are going to cast us out, send us into the herd of pigs." And He said to them, "Go!" And they came out and went into the pigs; and behold, the whole herd rushed down the steep bank into the sea and drowned in the waters. And the herdsmen ran away, and went to the city and reported everything, including what had happened to the demon-possessed men. And behold, the whole city came out to meet Jesus; and when they saw Him, they pleaded with Him to leave their region. (Matthew 8:28–34)

When Alexander the Great conquered that area, he set up what was called the Decapolis, the ten cities. On the eastern side of the Sea of Galilee, you have a Greek group of city-states. All of them are east of the Jordan and what is today the country of Jordan, except for a city called Beth-Shan that's on the west side. One of the cities is called Gerasa as in the Gerasene demoniac. When Jesus said, "Let's go to the other side," it meant "let's go to the Gentiles." It is believed this is a picture of the book of Acts. The Twelve launched out and there are great adversities, and Jesus calmed the winds and the waves on the way to the other side.

When you read the book of Acts, in the same way there is great adversity over the Twelve as they head to the Gentiles for the gospel. He went to the other side, the Decapolis, and here we are going to see the classic Gentile. When you think of a Greek, you think of the classic culture. The Greeks were the first to turn away from gods to look to human reason. It was better than gods. It wasn't as good as divine revelation but it was where we begin to see a rational culture, that was later absorbed by the Roman Empire whose quest was answered by Christianity that spread to form what is known as the Judeo-Christian Western worldview.

That's why when you go to a college, you join a Greek fraternity to enrich you in culture (feel free to laugh). We're going to see in the classic culture, the Gentile culture, a man of the city, "of the Decapolis." He's going to be pretty ugly. It's a picture of the Gentile world. Remember, when God told Abraham to raise a nation—"And in your seed all the nations of the earth shall be blessed" (Genesis 22:18)? That seed was Christ.

Abraham and Israel began in Genesis 12. What happened in Genesis 11? The Tower of Babel, where you saw a revolt against God after the flood. God confused their language. They separated and spread out, they intermarried and became the nations and the races that adopt their own religions. They ultimately became violent and perverse and idolatrous. That's how God sees the nations. They are spawned from rebellion. They have no God, only idols. They become just like the demoniac.

In effect, God said, "In your seed, Abraham, shall the nations be blessed. Because I'm going to send your seed,

Jesus Christ, to the Germans and the French and the Italians and the Norwegians and the Finns and the Russians and Africa and America and all these places, and Christ is going to be redemptive to a world full of crazy demon-possessed peoples." That's how God sees the coming history. Here in Matthew 8, we're going to look at the man without God. He will look very familiar. Number one, he was a demoniac. Satan conquered him. The Bible says "the whole world lies in the power of the evil one" (1 John 5:19). Satan had him. As a result, the name of the demon that speaks called himself "Legion."

When you hear the word *legion*, what do you think of? The Roman legion. But it's not Rome that is going to conquer this man. It is the devil. The Bible says Christ "rescued us from the domain of darkness" (Colossians 1:13). The Lord Jesus told Paul at his conversion that he will open people's eyes "so that they may turn from darkness to light, and from the power of Satan to God" (Acts 26:18). Paul said we were dead in our transgressions and sins in which we formally walked "according to the course of this world, according to the prince of the power of the air" (Ephesians 2:2). Satan has "blinded the minds of the unbelieving so that they will not see the light of the gospel of the glory of Christ, who is the image of God" (2 Corinthians 4:4).

Jesus said He came into the strong man's house to bind the strong man and then take away His possessions. Who is the strong man who owns the house? Satan. Who are his possessions? Mankind. That's the picture the Bible has of our world. It has been conquered by "the god of this world." Will that preach on CNN? Would that preach in Congress?

Imagine . . . "I would like to tell you all about the bondage of the devil you're all under." They would consider you crazy! The Bible never blinks as to who is the one over this world—"The whole world lies in the power of the evil one" (1 John 5:19).

All these religions, all these political and philosophical ideas, you can trace back to one person—"the father of lies"—because they're all antithetical to Yahweh the true God. "God told Adam concerning the tree of the knowledge of good and evil, 'On the day that you eat of it you will certainly die.'" Man was cut loose from God on the day Adam transgressed. Man became like an astronaut on a spacewalk. Cut the tether and he is sucked into the black darkness. I don't care what human-originated religion, psychology, sociology, philosophy, economy is, it's going to be anti-God and it's going to be painful.

Let's look at Luke 8:26–28:

> *Then they sailed to the country of the*
> *Gerasenes, which is opposite Galilee. And when*
> *He stepped out onto the land, a man from the*
> *city met Him who was possessed with demons;*
> *and he had not put on clothing for a long time*
> *and was not living in a house, but among the*
> *tombs. And seeing Jesus, he cried out and fell*
> *down before Him, and said with a loud voice,*
> *"What business do You have with me, Jesus,*
> *Son of the Most High God? I beg You, do not*
> *torment me!"*

The man had not put on any clothing. He was naked. He had no modesty or shame. He had no sense of decorum or decency. He had no sense of the dignity of the human body.

When a nation is alienated from God, the first thing you see is a loss of decency. What it will say publicly, what it will do publicly. Thus man is socially ostracized. He can't co-exist with any other humans. He only has one friend and it's another insane man. Matthew's account also tells you he was extremely violent. Why was he violent? He doesn't know, but it says "no one could pass by that way" (Matthew 8:28). If you got into his space and he would try to kill you. Is that the nature of man? Yes.

If you ever go down in the city, make sure your eyes don't meet another man's eyes because it could be seen as a challenge. Make sure you don't bump them. Make sure you don't crowd their space. Why will they get violent? Just because you're there, that's why. No one can pass that way. The man had taken an area of his culture and he commandeered it for the devil. Another thing about him in Luke 8:27, he was not living in a house, but among the tombs. He was the walking dead. Just as man is dead to God, society, himself, and his fellow man.

Man by himself cannot exist. Animals are hardwired, they have to do what they do. That's why you can't write a book on the history of the cheetah. They can never change. They must do what they do. Can you write a book on the history of man, though? Yes. You go into Dark Ages, Renaissance, Reformation, modernism, world war. Man can either be demonic or he can be angelic. He has choices but his will has been severed toward good. Another point about this tomb-dweller—he was alone. Alienated. He had no friends.

In the twentieth century the idea of *atomization* was heralded. A-T-O-M-ization—meaning, you're nothing but matter. You're just atoms. You can't say to anyone today that man is in the image of God. You can't say man understands where the universe comes from, that he has ultimate meaning. A book was written in the '70s called *The Lonely Crowd*. Such is man—miserable. Jean-Paul Sartre said man is a bubble of nothingness and a sea of emptiness. That's the message of twentieth-century thinkers. Misery. The Gospel of Mark says the man is crying in agony day and night. He is emotionally, socially, spiritually living in a world of broken glass.

Also, according to Mark's Gospel, he is also self-destructive.

> *They came to the other side of the sea, into the region of the Gerasenes. When He got out of the boat, immediately a man from the tombs with an unclean spirit met Him. He lived among the tombs; and no one was able to bind him anymore, not even with a chain, because he had often been bound with shackles and chains, and the chains had been torn apart by him and the shackles broken in pieces; and no one was strong enough to subdue him. Constantly, night and day, he was screaming among the tombs and in the mountains, and cutting himself with stones.* (Mark 5:1–5)

This possessed man was taking stones and gashing himself because Satan was in control. The thief comes, says John 10:10, "to rob, to kill, and to destroy." "Your adversary the devil prowls about like a roaring lion, seeking someone to devour" (1 Peter 5:8). "Man is born for trouble, as sparks fly upward" (Job 5:7). It's inevitable. How many of you have a loved one who is on a toboggan to hell and they continually shoot off all their toes, their feet, their hands? And the longer they live the more deranged they become. That's man. He's the prodigal, the prodigious, the excessive son.

And the demoniac was not just destructive; he was without rest. Mark says day and night he was exhausted. But Jesus says, "Come to Me, all who are weary and burdened and I will give you rest. Take My yoke upon you and learn from Me, for I am gentle and humble in heart, and you will find rest for your souls" (Matthew 11:28–29). Man also has been chained. All you can do with him is damage control. Chain him and put him under guard and maybe we can keep him from destroying himself and killing somebody else. Can they fix him? They can't. What about religion? Rules, philosophy, psychology, sociology, the threat of punishment, will that fix him? How about government aid? How about education? How about money and pleasure? There's nothing we can do to change man's heart. This man breaks all the chains you put on him. There's no vaccine for him. Man is conceived in sin and brought forth in iniquity. Just as the day we're currently in. We are merely patching the problem.

There's two words never mentioned when you watch the news. But until they're mentioned, it won't get fixed. We never talk about the real problem, and we never talk about the only solution. Until you say the word *sin* and until you mention the word *Christ* and His redemption, we're not going to fix man. The only way we can be fixed is by the grace of God. Our sin was dealt with through the mediation of Jesus Christ. So try to go down on the city square and preach that. People will not let you finish. Two things you can't say publicly in our country: sin and Christ.

Absolute wrong and absolute right—you can't talk about. You can talk G-O-D all you want to, but He can't be Yahweh, the God of the Bible. Man will break all the chains. There is only one thing this demon will bow before . . . *Jesus*. The man cried out and he fell before Him.

> *. . . and shouting with a loud voice, he said, "What business do You have with me, Jesus, Son of the Most High God? I implore You by God, do not torment me! For He had already been saying to him, "Come out of the man, you unclean spirit!" And He was asking him, "What is your name?" And he said to Him, "My name is Legion, for we are many." And he begged Him earnestly not to send them out of the region. Now there was a large herd of pigs feeding nearby on the mountain. And the demons begged Him, saying, "Send us into the pigs so that we may enter them.". . . and the herd rushed down the steep bank into the sea, about two thousand of them; and they were drowned in the sea.* (Mark 5:7–13)

How many knees will bow? "*Every knee* will bow . . . and every tongue will confess that Jesus Christ is Lord. . . . of those who are in heaven and on earth and under the earth [the demonic realm]" (Philippians 2:10–11, emphasis added). The demon assumes the position. He has to. He is in the presence of his Creator. Even the devil is God's devil.

Did the demon know why Jesus was there? "Have You come to torment us?" Did he know when it will be? The demon added in Matthew 8:29, "before the time." He even made a request not to command them to go into the abyss. Because the demon *knew* his final destination. The demon *knew* the power of Jesus.

As a matter of fact, he knew he *couldn't stay* unless Christ said. And he *couldn't go* unless Christ said. So the demons begged Jesus to send then to the pigs (Luke 8:32). It's a bit of irony. The man was bound, but when Christ arrived, who's bound? The demons. They couldn't do anything unless He said.

What nation cannot have pigs? Israel. They're a Gentile phenomenon. The pigs represent the collective Gentile society, the unclean. They are mindless, they are filthy, and they are savage.

Who did Christ say you better not throw your pearls in front of (see Matthew 7:6)? Swine, because they want peas, not pearls. When they realize they don't have something for their bodies, they'll turn on you. It's like man. Man doesn't want anything spiritual. He just wants something financial. He just wants another cut of meat. They're also self-destructive. It's what Satan does. He gets in them, and they head downhill to their death. When you go downhill, you go faster and faster and faster until you're out of control and end up in the abyss.

Pigs follow each other blindly because that's what makes the pig a pig. It does what it does because everybody else does it. Man, darkened to God, mindless, goes downhill on his way to hell because everybody around him is motivated by Satan. Those are the nations. But the demoniac? Once he is healed, when the demons have gone, he is sitting down at the feet of Jesus, clothed and in his right mind.

How quickly is he healed? Instantly.

Twas grace that taught my heart to fear and grace
    my fear relieved.
How precious did that grace appear the hour I
    first believed?—"Amazing Grace"

I have a close friend named Tommy. He and his wife, Lee, trusted Christ with me at a dinner table years ago. He was going away on a business trip, and Lee met him on the trip. She asked, "Do you feel different?" Tommy replied, "I do." She said, "I do too." Tommy continued, "I feel clean." Lee agreed and said, "I feel whole, I've come together." That's salvation. The bondage is broken.

The previously demon-possessed man was now under a Savior, a new Lord—Jesus Christ. The man was seated, at rest, and clothed. He was no longer indecent; he was socially acceptable and at the feet of Jesus. He was listening and in his right mind. Not a different mind merely, he was in his *right* mind. He could see and *know* the way things ought to be.

When Adam was created, Adam saw God, who made Himself known to him. In the light of God, he saw the universe, himself, his body, the animals, nature, the air he breathed. He understood Eve, his wife. "This is bone of my bone." He understood his purpose. He knew not to eat of this, but to eat of that. Right and wrong. Everything made sense to Adam because he understood God. When you get rid of God, you're in the dark in all things.

But we need to also notice the crowd in Luke 8—rather than be joyful of how a demon-possessed man was made well, the crowd became frightened. All the people of the country and the surrounding district asked Jesus to leave. When Christ arrived, everything was upside down. Demons were in control; a man was destroyed. A city was under a threat. Within seconds, the demons and pigs were gone, the man was in his right mind, everything was set right. The crowd should have been praising God with hallelujahs! They should have done what the French did when the Americans went into Paris—celebrate! But the crowd said, "Get out of here." Why? Because Jesus fixed things and people who were more important than pigs and money. Does that still scare man? The story is prophetic.

The last thing you see about the former demoniac is his begging Jesus that he might accompany Him (Luke 8:38). It's a touching scene. After the man jumped in the boat, I imagine they began counting heads, and it numbered fourteen. One extra. "What are *you* doing here?" the Twelve may have asked. "I want to go with you and tell others," he replies. Why? He has found the solution. This guy in about a ten-minute period went from being the problem to being part of the solution,

Jesus responded to his request with the command, "Return to *your home* and describe what great things God has done for you" (8:39, emphasis added). Does God ever say no to us? "I have something better." My life has been wonderfully guided by "no's" as well as "yeses."

In the Gospel of Matthew, Jesus came back to that area later on and they all came out to Him because of the testimony of this man. Why am I writing in such detail on the demoniac when this book is about God and country? The stories relate. Our country and world have gone mad. We have always been mad, but we were influenced by the light and salt of the Church. Has the knowledge of the Bible been rejected scientifically, philosophically, morally, and rationally? Yes. Because it didn't work? Rather, because it did. And Christ brings change. Just like in the Decapolis. Does this demoniac look familiar? Looks like an American.

Jesus is our only hope. Who has the knowledge of Him? The man who has partaken of Christ's goodness goes back into the city and stands up for Him. Without God, man will become indecent, then immoral, then violent, then despairing, and then he will go mad. Just like the demoniac.

This miracle is depictive of the Gentile world. Society can shackle and restrain us but we can break the chains. Our only hope is the One rejected by His people. From Jesus alone will Satan flee. But it is Him the world refuses and upon that refusal will plunge as a herd into the abyss. Faster and faster following the crowd. Listen to the man whose life was transformed. Listen to Christ's witnesses, seated at His feet.

This is the world of "the other side." It may look familiar. It looks like the madness of Nebuchadnezzar, King of Babylon (Daniel 4). Without God, *all* go mad. Man's only hope is Jesus. Such is God and country.

3

Sons of the Serpent

GENESIS 3:14–4:26

The LORD God said to the serpent, "Because you
have done this, cursed are you more than all
cattle, and more than every beast of the field;
on your belly you will go, and dust you will eat
all the days of your life; and I will put enmity
between you and the woman, and between your
seed and her seed; He shall bruise you on the
head, and you shall bruise him on the heel."
To the woman He said, "I will greatly multiply
your pain in childbirth, in pain you will bring
forth children; yet your desire will be for your
husband, and he will rule over you." Then to
Adam He said, "Because you have listened to
the voice of your wife, and have eaten from the
tree about which I commanded you, saying,
'You shall not eat from it'; cursed is the ground
because of you; in toil you will eat of it all the

*days of your life. Both thorns and thistles it
shall grow for you; and you will eat the plants
of the field; by the sweat of your face you will
eat bread, till you return to the ground, because
from it you were taken; for you are dust, and to
dust you shall return." Now the man called his
wife's name Eve, because she was the mother of
all the living. The* LORD *God made garments of
skin for Adam and his wife, and clothed them.*

Then the LORD *God said, "Behold, the
man has become like one of Us, knowing good
and evil; and now, he might stretch out his
hand, and take also from the tree of life, and
eat, and live forever"—therefore the* LORD *God
sent him out of the garden of Eden, to cultivate
the ground from which he was taken. So He
drove the man out; and at the east of the garden
of Eden He stationed the cherubim and the
flaming sword which turned every direction to
guard the way to the tree of life.*

*Now the man had relations with his wife
Eve, and she conceived and gave birth to Cain,
and she said, "I have gotten a man child with
the help of the* LORD.*" Again, she gave birth
to his brother Abel. And Abel was a keeper of
flocks, but Cain was a tiller of the ground. So
it came about in the course of time that Cain*

brought an offering to the LORD *of the fruit of the ground. Abel, on his part also brought of the firstlings of his flock and of their fat portions. And the* LORD *had regard for Abel and for his offering; but for Cain and for his offering He had no regard. So Cain became very angry and his countenance fell. Then the* LORD *said to Cain, "Why are you angry? And why has your countenance fallen? If you do well, will not your countenance be lifted up? And if you do not do well, sin is crouching at the door; and its desire is for you, but you must master it." Cain told Abel his brother. And it came about when they were in the field, that Cain rose up against Abel his brother and killed him.*

Then the LORD *said to Cain, "Where is Abel your brother?" And he said, "I do not know. Am I my brother's keeper?" He said, "What have you done? The voice of your brother's blood is crying to Me from the ground. Now you are cursed from the ground, which has opened its mouth to receive your brother's blood from your hand. When you cultivate the ground, it will no longer yield its strength to you; you will be a vagrant and a wanderer on the earth." Cain said to the* LORD, *"My punishment is too great to bear! Behold, You have driven me this day from the* face of the ground; and from Your face I will be hidden, and I will be a vagrant and a wanderer on the earth, and whoever finds me will kill me." So the LORD said to him, "Therefore whoever kills Cain, vengeance will be taken on him sevenfold." And the LORD appointed a sign for Cain, so that no one finding him would slay him.

Then Cain went out from the presence of the LORD, and settled in the land of Nod, east of Eden. Cain had relations with his wife and she conceived, and gave birth to Enoch; and he built a city, and called the name of the city Enoch, after the name of his son. Now to Enoch was born Irad, and Irad became the father of Mehujael, and Mehujael became the father of Methushael, and Methushael became the father of Lamech. Lamech took to himself two wives: the name of the one was Adah, and the name of the other, Zillah. Adah gave birth to Jabal; he was the father of those who dwell in tents and have livestock. His brother's name was Jubal; he was the father of all those who play the lyre and pipe. As for Zillah, she also gave birth to Tubal-cain, the forger of all implements of bronze and iron; and the sister of Tubal-cain was Naamah. Lamech said to his wives,

"Adah and Zillah, listen to my voice, you wives of Lamech, give heed to my speech, for I have killed a man for wounding me; and a boy for striking me; if Cain is avenged sevenfold, then Lamech seventy-sevenfold." Adam had relations with his wife again; and she gave birth to a son, and named him Seth, for, she said, "God has appointed me another offspring in place of Abel, for Cain killed him." To Seth, to him also a son was born; and he called his name Enosh. Then men began to call upon the name of the LORD.

When you back away and look at the Bible's narrative, you notice it has bookends. An Alpha and an Omega. Eden and the New Jerusalem. Genesis 1 and Revelation 22. Creation and the New Creation. The parenthesis in between is the mess man has made of things. Let me show you what God has said about the present world we live in.

Many people wonder in the days we are in, how are you supposed to live the Christian life when everything looks like the wheels are coming off? They've *always* been in a state of repair. We're still focusing on God and country, but just stay with me as we take a look back at Genesis. "The beginning." If you know Genesis, the rest of your Bible is a footnote.

When I do my Young Guns Discipleship program with the men who come to Denton, Texas, for a year's study, all I do for four months is teach them Genesis. If I teach you Genesis, I've got you. Then I show you Matthew. Then I show you Romans. I show you Revelation, and you've got your head around your Bible. Genesis is broken into two parts. Chapter 12–50 is the *national* section because it's talking about Israel. About Abraham, then Isaac, then Jacob, then Joseph.

Israel is a solution to the debacle of Genesis 1–11: the *universal* section. The Bible doesn't begin with Israel. We don't get to Israel until chapter 12, with Abraham, the father of the Jews.

Chapters 1–11 are called "the planks." What if I were to ask you, What are the foundational ideas of human existence? You might say: Where does the *creation* come from? That's pretty foundational. What is *man*? Where did *evil* come from? What is evil's *remedy*? Also, *civilization*—the place where we come together. Greece, Rome, Persia, Babylon, the United States, Germany, College Station, all these different places. Where does civilization come from? The good guys and the bad guys.

How about *judgment*? Will God ever judge civilization? How about the *nations* and races and religions? What I just gave you in a brief paragraph is Genesis 1–11.

- Genesis 1, God of the *creation*
- Genesis 2, *man* in the image of God
- Chapter 3, *the fall* of man
- Chapter 3:16, where *redemption* comes from; the seed of woman who crushes the serpent
- In chapters 4 and 5 we see *civilization*, the seed of the serpent and the seed of the woman, the bad guys and the good guys.

- Chapters 6–9, *judgment* in the flood of Noah.
- Chapters 10 and 11, the Tower of Babel and the *nations* that came forth from its rebellion
- And then in Genesis 12, the solution to the fall. Abraham, the nation of Israel, and Abraham's seed— the Messiah. "In your seed shall the nations be blessed."

That's worth the price of admission right there. Those are the planks. What I want to camp on in this chapter is chapters 4 and 5, that of civilization. The word "city" gets mentioned for the first time in Genesis 4. What does the city look like? It looks like it is cursed. In chapter 3:14, after the fall of man we have the first time another word is mentioned: "cursed."

God speaks to the serpent and Satan the one behind the serpent. "Cursed are you more than all cattle." Then we see a judgment on nature, the family, the animal realm, man, woman, the human race, and on man working by the sweat of his brow. ". . . you are dust, and to dust, you shall return" (Genesis 3:19). There is physical death.

Genesis 3 and 4 looks at *the results* of the curse. Evil isn't something within the nature of God. It is not within the creation. There is no yin and yang, no good force, bad force. The origin of evil is rebellion against God. Where will the solution for evil come from? In Genesis 3:15 God only waits one sentence after the word "curse" before He gives the remedy to man's sin.

God says to the serpent, "I'll put enmity," which is a word meaning instinctive hatred, "between you and the woman, between your seed, and her seed." The serpent has seed? Satan has children? He does. Who does the Bible call the seed of the devil? There is a people in the Bible where it is said of them they're "conceived in sin and brought forth in iniquity."

There is a people about whom it is said, "you were dead in your trespasses and sins in which you formally walked according to the course of this world, according to the prince of the power of the air, of the spirit that is now working in the *sons of* disobedience" (Ephesians 2:1–2). Who are we talking about? Human beings. Natural-born humans, sinners. There's a reason. Our nature. Our hearts.

We are conceived in sin and brought forth in iniquity. That's the nature of man. He is not the *tabula rasa* of John Locke. He is not the noble savage of Rousseau. There's something wrong with us. Jesus said to the Pharisees in John 8:44, "You are of your father the devil." We're from "the domain of darkness." God told Paul he would turn men from "the power of Satan to God" (Acts 26:18). Natural-born humans are alien to God. Genesis 3:15 continues, "your seed and *her seed*." What does that mean? What is this "seed of woman"?

"He"—a singular male pronoun. "He" is "the seed of the woman." "*He* shall bruise you on the head." When you see a venomous snake, what do you do? You step on him and kill him. Satan is going to be defeated by a singular *Person*, and it's not going to be you or me. It's not going to be religion. It's not going to be politics. It's not going to be education. It's not going to be science and medicine. The sin issue will be solved by a Man who's going to become one of us, and His victory will be the victory of those who trust in Him.

Who's the Man? Jesus, the seed of woman. "At the fullness of the time," Paul said, "God sent forth His son born of a woman." Never, ever in the Bible do you trace a man through his mother. You always trace him through his father—except right here. Why? If you're born a sinner, how can you be a Savior? By a miraculous way, Jesus's birth is going to circumvent a natural birth—born of a virgin! There are two races, the only races the Bible recognizes. Those fathered by Satan. His seed are born physically through Adam, man's federal head. And those who are born spiritually through Christ the last Adam.

At birth we are "natural" men. We are spiritually dead. You can talk to men all day about God and they can't follow you nor do they care, and if you tell them what you mean, they'll get mad at you, because they're dead to God. Alien. Enemies. They're alive to the lust of the flesh, the lust of the eyes, and the pride of life, but not to God.

What Adam did is imputed to all of us, and what Christ "the seed of woman" did is imputed to all of us who are in Christ. We received what Adam did in our nature, and we are fallen. We received what Christ did, His righteousness, and we are now "spiritual men." We are born again. We're alive to God. To be a child of the devil, you simply need a physical birth; to be a child of God, you need a new birth, a spiritual birth.

Just as Israel sat in terror against Goliath, until one man faced him and killed him and cut off his head with his own sword, we have a David who faced Goliath. Jesus.

His name will be called "the Lord," because He is God. "Jesus," because He became a man. And in His office He is the Christ. "The *Lord Jesus Christ.*"

Genesis 3:15 is foreshadowing that humanity will be saved by a Man who will defeat sin, yet He will have to give His life, "the serpent shall wound His heel." Through the rest of the Bible, we can trace this Man from the seed of woman, to Noah, to Shem and the Semitic people to Abraham, Isaac, Jacob, Judah, Bethlehem, Jesse, David, Joseph, "the husband of Mary, by whom Jesus was born" (Matthew 1:16).

But now let's turn to Genesis 4:1. The first two sons of Adam and Eve are depictive of these two races. First John 3:10 says, "By this *the children of God* and the *children of the devil* are obvious." For this reason, Cain killed Abel (v. 12). Cain and Abel are seen as the mouths of two rivers and their actions are depictive of all humanity to follow.

In chapter 4, Adam had relations with his wife, Eve, and she conceived and gave birth to Cain. She said, "I have gotten a manchild with the help of the Lord." She's hoping this boy is the one. The seed of woman that will bring redemption from the fall. Is this him? By the second born we know it is not.

In verse 2, she gave birth to Abel. Abel means "vanity" or "futility." The first child she had hopes for, then she realizes, "vanity." Eve has recognized our race is fallen. Salvation is not going to come through man.

Cain depicts Adam *after* the fall. Abel is a depiction of man *prior* to the fall. Abel was a keeper of flocks as Adam was told to rule the creation. After the fall, man will work by the sweat of his brow. He is outside of Eden and laboring in a cursed earth. And so Cain is a tiller of the ground.

We're looking at the mouth of the rivers. "It came about in the course of time" (v. 3) that Cain brought an offering to the Lord of the fruit of the ground. Abel brought an offering from the firstlings of his flock. Why did they bring an offering? Well, recall when Adam and Eve tried to cover themselves to hide after they had sinned. God provided a covering for them—an animal, probably a lamb, was sacrificed by God, and Adam and Eve were covered by the blood of the Lamb. That act of atonement now becomes an institution of sacrifice.

In verse 4, "Abel . . . brought the firstlings of his flock." The Lord literally "looked with favor" on Abel and his offering (NIV). For Cain and his offering, He did not look; He turned away from it. Abel brought a sacrifice—something had to die through the shedding of blood. Cain brought the works of his hands; he tore up some barley and threw it down.

As a result, God accepts one and He doesn't accept the other. He refuses the works of our hands. This is the gospel call. What He *will* accept is obedience to the revealed will of God and the testimony of God of trusting in One who will die for you. "You, I will take. You, I will not." Let's watch Cain's response. It is every man's response. It is the response of the children of the dark to being told they can't get to heaven on their own.

Sinners can only enter heaven by the activity of God on their behalf. Do men have a problem with that? You bet they do. In verse 5, Cain became very angry. Men don't like the stumbling block of Christ. "All our righteous acts are like filthy rags" (Isaiah 64:6 NIV). No man will come to the

Father except by the blood of the Lamb. The tabernacle of God, is 150 feet wide. How big is the entrance? It's about 30 feet wide, like God spreading His arms. But you have to go through something narrow. A turnstile.

It's a sacrificial altar. If you don't come that way, you die. Cain didn't like that. It's a stumbling block. It's a stone of stumbling and a rock of offense and Cain's countenance fell. He was very unhappy, as he did not like to be told he was a moral failure. No one does. In verse 6, he is confronted by God, "Why are you angry? Why has your countenance fallen? If you do well"— meaning, repent of your self-righteousness, and your haughty attitude to God—"will not your countenance be lifted up?"

God warns Cain in verse 7 that if he doesn't do what is right, sin will consume him. This is the first mention of the word "sin" in the Bible, and it is likened to a predator. "Sin is crouching at your door, and its desire is for you." Meaning, "You're not going to cohabit with sin. You master it or it will devour you." This is the way we had better treat the devil. He's not going to cohabit with us; he longs to consume us.

Would you repent if God rebuked you and told you to repent? Let's see what Cain did. God's counseling appointment didn't go well. Cain told Abel his brother, "I'm really your pal. Come with me" (see v. 8). This is similar to how the Pharisees wanted to get Jesus alone so they could arrest Him and execute Him. "He told Abel his brother. And it came about when they were in the field . . ." You know why Cain gets him in the field? Because he thinks God can't see him now.

"Cain rose up against Abel his brother and killed him," because Cain had contempt for God, he had contempt for the sacrifice, he had contempt for the shedding of blood, contempt for the Word of God, and contempt for the people of God. "If I can't have my way, I will remove the light that illumines me." Does Cain look familiar? It's natural man. The seed of the serpent that was foretold by God. The book of Jude says of evil men "they have gone the way of Cain" (Jude 11).

If one rejects the restraint of sin, there is no place sin will stop. There is nothing a human can't do. In verse 9, God confronted Cain. "'Where is Abel your brother?' And he said, 'I do not know.'" That's called a lie. He now held God in contempt. His anger at Abel worked its way back to Abel's God. "Am I my brother's keeper?" Abel was a keeper of the flocks, a good shepherd. "I don't like God, and I don't like His good shepherd and I don't like that cross and I don't like that bloody sacrifice. I don't like to be told I'm not acceptable. I sure don't like to be told Abel is and I'm not." Sound familiar? "If I can't get rid of God, then I'm going to get rid of you." That's man. How many people died in the communist regime from 1917 to 1989? 100 million. In Russia, they were killing 5,000 a day in political executions. All because many did not agree with the atheism of Marxism. What can man not descend to?

If you know your history, you know of the French Revolution, the Russian Revolution, and the Chinese Revolution which destroyed anyone who disagreed with their atheistic decrees. There is *nothing* restricting men without God.

In verse 10, God confronted Cain. "What have you done? The voice of your brother's blood is crying to Me from the ground." God shows mercy. Cain should have died, but God said, "You are cursed from the ground." God's going to make him an example. The book of Numbers says, "Murder pollutes the land" (35:33). Nature and life will chasten Cain.

"I'm going to bring a judgment on you and all the world is going to look at you and know what you have done. You are going to be a vagrant. I'm going to show the world what happens to someone who rejects the atonement. Who rejects the Good Shepherd, God and His sacrifice: life will punish them" (see vv. 11–12). Sinners think they're going to have utopia once they are free from God.

Do you know what the word *utopia* means? It means "no place." That's utopia. There is a place described in the Bible where there is no mourning, crying, sickness, or pain. Where is that? Heaven. In verse 12, "When you cultivate the ground, it will no longer yield its strength." That's the coming story of civilization: barrenness and alienation.

Then Cain actually judged God! "My punishment is too great to bear! Behold, You have driven me this day from the face of the ground; and from Your face I will be hidden, and I will be a vagrant and a wanderer on the earth, and whoever finds me will kill me" (v. 13). I'm amazed the next verse does not say, "And behold fire came from heaven and consumed him." But what did God do? God showed Cain mercy. He said, "Whoever kills Cain, vengeance will be taken on him sevenfold" (v. 15). "The Lord is not slow about His promise, as some count slowness, but is patient toward you" (2 Peter 3:9).

God wants the world to see what happens when one renounces the true God. If God is dead, man is dead, and marriage is dead, and sexuality is dead, and civilization is dead, and government is dead, and the arts are dead. If man removes the marrow of life, all of civilization wastes to nothing.

Maybe this would be a good high school graduation message: You can be as smart as you want, have all the money you can have, and all the learning, but if you do not know the God of truth and cannot make a moral decision, you are a dead man walking. That's why philosophy is called the queen of sciences. It's the attempt to discern what is right and true. In verse 15, "God appointed" or literally "set a mark" for Cain. God did something seven generations later under Lamech that people remembered: "If Cain is avenged sevenfold, then Lamech seventy-sevenfold" (v. 24). What was the mark for Cain or perhaps "on Cain"?

May I give you a sanctified opinion? The idea is used also in Ezekiel 9 when an angel was sent through Israel prior to the judgment of the Babylonians, and God put "a mark" on the Jews who repented and He spared them. The word "mark" is a Hebrew letter—the letter "taw." You know what a taw looks like? It's a T—a cross. You're covered.

At the first Passover, the angel of death slayed the first-born except those who had a taw on the house. The sign of blood. A cross of blood. When Israel was bitten by the serpents, God erected a sign. To look to it saved them from the serpent. The sign was a bronze serpent, a representation of evil, placed on a standard. A taw.

So I think God gave Cain, in some sense, a cross. It's what Cain hid under.

In verse 16, "Cain went out from the presence of the LORD," because God in the area of Eden met with man much like a temple, a tabernacle, "and he settled in the land of Nod." Do you know that Nod means "wandering" in Hebrew? Whenever you don't know God, you are blowing in the wind. You're unanchored. There Cain settled. Now, in verse 17, we see the generations after him. What does civilization look like when you take a Cain, a seed of the serpent, and build a civilization?

When you look at it, it's going to look a whole lot like Seattle, LA, DC, Paris, Berlin, Moscow, and Dallas. "Cain had relations with his wife, she conceived and gave birth to Enoch. And he built a city, and named it after his son" (v. 17). Wander indeed! This is the first time the word "city" occurs in the Bible. Man masses. He doesn't like to live by himself. He can't get along with men, but man will mass into a great amount of men. Man can't help but be personal because he is in the image of God. But always in the Bible, the city is dangerous because you have lots of fallen human beings. When you want to retire, where do you most want to go? Brooklyn? Probably not. Cain builds a city because man is a political being and he wants to exist with other men. If you'll keep looking, in verse 18, you see the lineage of Adam: there's Adam and Cain, that's two. Then you have Enoch, that's three. To Enoch was born Irad, that's four; the father of Methujael, that's five. Methushael, that is six, father of Lamech, that is seven. We're looking at approximately 2,000 years right there in one verse.

You see that little suffix, -el in Methujael and Methushael. That -el suffix means God, "Elohim." Their names have the name of God. It's not the covenant name, "Yahweh" as in Elisha or Elijah. El is a generic name for a deity. Man is not just political, he is religious. He will always find a religion to try to give him final meaning and answers. It may not be the true God but a quasi-God, like a golden calf.

In the seventh generation is the man Lamech, which means something violent, "the conqueror." Let's see what happens to civilization over the years. Do you remember the maxim for the Unity Church? That man is getting "better every day and every way." In verse 19, Lamech took to himself two wives. A man leaves his father and mother and cleaves to his wife. One is the prescribed number of wives. Why would you have two wives? To have more kids to build your power base. Who gets the dirty end of the stick here? Woman. Wherever you don't see God, marriage is going to start being dishonored and women are always going to suffer. The men of Genesis 9 are political and religious and domestic. But marriage, womanhood, and sexuality are going downward in time.

In verse 20, "Adah [Lamech's wife] gave birth to Jabal; he was the father of those who dwell in tents and have livestock." What's that called? It's called agriculture. Man is going to still have the cultural mandate of subduing the creation and ruling it, but he's going to do it without God. "His brother's name was Jubal; he was the father of all those who play the lyre and pipe" (v. 21).

Artistically man is advancing; he is an artistic creature. He wants to be lifted up beyond the physical creation to sing and to have happiness. He's political. He's religious. He's domestic, agricultural, and artistic. Something else, Adah gave birth to Tubal-cain, the forger of implements of bronze and iron (v. 22).

Man has learned if he'll take a rock and fire it up and melt the ore out of it, he can let it cool and can make something that's better than stone. Man is industrious. He is scientific. He is into education, the transference of knowledge, and he is into industry. Again, the question: Is man going up? In culture, yes, he is. Is he going up in artistry? In technology, education? Yes, he's going up.

In verse 23, incidentally, that word, *Tubal-cain*, is believed to be preserved in mythology. In mythology, the god of the underworld is the one who works with fire and metal, Vulcan. Many have felt the name Tubal-cain would be played on later as the name Vulcan. It's interesting how mythology will often reflect the real truth of Genesis carried on in stories just like the flood narrative in the *Gilgamesh* epic. In verse 23, Lamech said to his wives, "Adah and Zillah, listen to my voice, you wives of Lamech, give heed to my speech, for I have killed a man for wounding me; and a boy for striking me." He is now proud of what earlier was the offense of murder and he boasts about how violent he is. Man is going up in society and in civilization, but going down in the dignity of man.

Cain's example is remembered 2,000 years later in verse 24: "If Cain is avenged sevenfold. Lamech seventy-seven." But does the fear of God limit Lamech's sin? Not at all. Lamech's words meant, "Don't be afraid of God. You need to be afraid of me." Man has gone up in civilization.

He's gone down in theology and the fear of God in his home, in the dignity of women, in the dignity of men, in the dignity of a boy smaller than he and now he boasts of his contempt of God. God and men mean nothing to him.

Genesis 4 shows you what man is going to look like. Often in the Bible at the beginning of an epoch, you'll have a signature event by God. For instance, Abraham offering up his son Isaac. God doesn't make every man do that, but the initial father of the faith had to do it. It's a lesson. And that's what this is. God was saying, in effect, "This is civilization and this is what's going to happen to it." My point is, *man cannot be ruled without God*. You'll notice the covenant name of God is not mentioned from Cain. The Lord is forgotten. They are secular humanists but man can't exist in a family, in a society, and in a political culture without God. You will either go one of two ways. One way is totalitarian rule— think Hitler or Mussolini. It's called fascism. The other way is you give power to the people. You let the people decide what is right.

Back in France in the 1700s, you had an enormous inequity between the wealthy and the poor. Most of us remember Marie Antoinette. When they said to her, "The people have no bread," she said, "If they have no bread, let them eat cake." (You don't want to say that to a bunch of poor people.) They replied, "How about we cut your head off?" The common man took over and the wealthy were killed.

What should they have done in France? They should have gone back to the Word of God. They should have had a reformation, but they didn't. They were progressive and invented a means of jurisprudence that had never existed.

A fellow named Rousseau rejected the notion of the innate sin of man that Calvin taught. Rousseau said, "Man is not a sinner. The problem with man is that he has too much pressure on him through society, through rules, and particularly, through the church. Just get rid of the rules. Man is 'the noble savage.' In time he will flourish if we can just remove the rules binding him."

Rousseau didn't want to be bound. He was a true child of nature—born to be wild.

His thought was this: "Because man is inherently good, he needs to get away from government, kings and priests." He said, "The voice of the people is the voice of God." The people gathered and stormed the Bastille. Then they said, "We're going to get rid of the ruling class." If you were aristocratic, if you were from wealth, or if you had anything to do with the church, you were guilty. "I don't *feel* guilty?" "You are by what you are born and you've got to die." It's called systemic racism. Today it is called cultural Marxism.

They had to get something to be merciful for death, so a doctor called Dr. Guillotin found a way to chop your head off. They killed systematically anyone who was part of the demographic that the revolutionaries decreed to be systematically prejudiced. They got rid of them, as did China, as did Stalin, as did Castro. They rearranged history to teach history differently. They censored books, had book burnings.

After a while, the revolutionaries turned on each other and they killed each other. When principles are rejected, when the pack brings bloodshed, you will always have a predator to take over. Who did Russia have? Stalin. Who did France have? Napoleon. Germany had Hitler. Cuba had

Castro. You'll always have a king of the beasts when law breaks down. Why do I say that? That's where we are right now. And the cry is that of systemic racism, "the voice of the people." The voice now is, "The problem is the white, male, heterosexual native-born, cisgender." They are guilty when they're born. To the degree you differentiate from them, you are now the oppressed. "I don't feel oppressed." "Yes, but you are to the degree that you are not one of them, they are the bad guys and they have to go." Just recently we were burning everything down and threatening peace officers. We're having shades of a French revolution. It will always happen when God is scorned.

Genesis 4 is a *plank* of reality. It is what all society looks like when alienated from God. It is prophetic of where all society is headed. Chapter 4 forms the world God will remove through the flood. Violence will always commandeer a culture that has abandoned God. The culture may advance in all physical aspects but in those things separating it from the jungle, that culture will wither. Men without God will always go "the way of Cain." Sons of the serpent.

Such is God and country. Our country. All countries.

4

Seed of the Woman

GENESIS 4:25–5:32

Adam had relations with his wife again, and she gave birth to a son, and named him Seth, for, she said, "God has appointed me another child in place of Abel, because Cain killed him." To Seth also a son was born; and he named him Enosh. Then people began to call upon the name of the LORD.

This is the book of the generations of Adam. On the day when God created man, He made him in the likeness of God. He created them male and female, and He blessed them and named them "mankind" on the day when they were created.

When Adam had lived 130 years, he fathered a son in his own likeness, according to his image, and named him Seth. Then the days of Adam after he fathered Seth were eight hundred years, and he fathered other sons and daughters. So all the days that Adam lived were 930 years, and he died.

Now Seth lived 105 years, and fathered Enosh. Then Seth lived 807 years after he fathered Enosh, and he fathered other sons and daughters. So all the days of Seth were 912 years, and he died.

Now Enosh lived ninety years, and fathered Kenan. Then Enosh lived 815 years after he fathered Kenan, and he fathered other sons and daughters. So all the days of Enosh were 905 years, and he died.

Now Kenan lived seventy years, and fathered Mahalalel. Then Kenan lived 840 years after he fathered Mahalalel, and he fathered other sons and daughters. So all the days of Kenan were 910 years, and he died.

Now Mahalalel lived sixty-five years, and fathered Jared. Then Mahalalel lived 830 years after he fathered Jared, and he fathered other sons and daughters. So all the days of Mahalalel were 895 years, and he died.

Now Jared lived 162 years, and fathered Enoch. Then Jared lived eight hundred years after he fathered Enoch, and he fathered other

sons and daughters. So all the days of Jared were
962 years, and he died.

Now Enoch lived sixty-five years, and
fathered Methuselah. Then Enoch walked
with God three hundred years after he fathered
Methuselah, and he fathered other sons and
daughters. So all the days of Enoch were 365
years. Enoch walked with God; and he was not,
for God took him.

Now Methuselah lived 187 years, and
fathered Lamech. Then Methuselah lived 782
years after he fathered Lamech, and he fathered
other sons and daughters. So all the days of
Methuselah were 969 years, and he died.

Now Lamech lived 182 years, and fathered
a son. And he named him Noah, saying, "This
one will give us comfort from our work and
from the hard labor of our hands caused by
the ground which the Lord has cursed." Then
Lamech lived 595 years after he fathered Noah,
and he fathered other sons and daughters. So
all the days of Lamech were 777 years, and he
died.

Now after Noah was five hundred years
old, Noah fathered Shem, Ham, and Japheth.

In 1980, just before John Lennon was assassinated, he said, "Weren't the '70's a drag." He was right. But he had no hope. He could only "imagine." Life without God is indeed a drag. But the seed of woman, the children of God headed by our last Adam can do far more than "imagine." Genesis 4 was painful to watch. But in chapter 5, there is light.

Let me begin it with this. I have a friend named Bill Burnett who played running back at Arkansas. He started there for three years and he told me once, "Whenever you put on that red at Arkansas and hear 'Ooooo Pig! Sooey!'" he said, "It's worth ten points." And so it is with the child of God. He's *somebody*. Somebody special.

So we are up ten points already when we understand who we are because we are part of something bigger than us.

In chapters 4 and 5 of Genesis, we look at civilization. We see civilization typified, in two races, represented by Cain and Abel. Chapter 4 revealed the seed of the serpent that will be destroyed by Christ. At the end of chapter 4, we saw the days of Lamech. In Lamech's day, the culture went up, in agriculture, up in the arts, up in technology, industry, and science.

In seven generations, the generation of Cain improved in the subduing of the earth. But they did it without the true God. They had amazing ability in the arts, in agriculture, livestock, technology, industry, but in the area of God, "I have killed a man for wounding me; and a boy for striking me. If Cain is avenged sevenfold, then Lamech seventy-sevenfold" (4:23–24). The fear of God went down. Their recognition of the word of God went down. Their sense of justice went down. Man in the image of God disappeared. The family order was fading away.

When you forget God, you're going to forget man. When God is dead, man is dead. That is typical of what was going to happen in Egypt and Syria, Babylon, Persia, Greece, and Rome and all civilizations. Man may walk on the moon and invent computers, but he can't keep from spousal abuse. He can't keep from being a sexual predator, a murderer, and mocker of God's judgment.

This is what the seed of the serpent looks like. It will keep going down until chapter 6 when God says, "Man has corrupted his way on the earth and his every thought is on violence. I'm going to destroy it" (see vv. 11–13). Will God let civilization go on forever like this? He will not. God will intervene again and deal with it.

And now in chapter 5, we are going to see *another* race. It's the seed of the woman to be headed by Christ. Not those simply born, but those who are reborn of God. The seed of the woman through Abel, the children of God.

A Christian should say of chapter 5, "they look very familiar." Chapter 5 had best look familiar to us because it's you and me we're going to be looking at. Alongside the pagan culture of chapter 4, chapter 5 elaborates on the seed of the woman.

In chapter 4:25, "Adam had relations with his wife again [after the death of Abel]; and she gave birth to a son and named him Seth ["appointed"—which is what Seth means], for she said, "God has appointed me another [seed] in place of Abel, for Cain killed him."

It is important to note Seth did not merely succeed Abel. Seth *replaced* Abel. There needed to be another man who took Abel's place as a righteous man to head the lineage of the seed of woman. There had to be another person like Abel who feared God, and that man was Seth. In other words, the righteous race needed a substitute to head it.

Does that sound familiar? The Christian has a substitute. Seth is a type of Jesus. These people know who they are. They are not of Cain, but are distinct, the people of God. I'm going to show you about thirteen things about these people.

In verse 26, "To Seth also a son was born; and he named him Enosh." Enosh is Hebrew for "frailty" or "weakness."

In contrast to Lamech, he was not one who had physical prowess. He was one with spiritual strength. And thus verse 26 says, "Then men began to call upon the name of the Lord." What does the Bible say about being saved? "Everyone who calls on the name of the Lord will be saved" (Acts 2:21). In his day you begin to see men, just like Abel, who put saving faith in sacrifice. It is not only Seth but all the lineage begins to call upon the name of the Lord.

This is the first time in the Bible we see prayer. And they called upon "the Lord." The line of Seth were the people who preserved the covenant name of "Lord" which was introduced in Genesis 2:4. This is a term also used concerning Abraham. In chapter 12 we see the call of Abraham. "Abram passed through the land [of Canaan] as far as the site of Shechem, to the Oak of Moreh" (12:6). There Abraham built an altar and "called upon the name of the Lord."

Abraham continued in the way of the chosen line. A way established by Seth.

The generation of Seth trusted, as they are "Enosh." They are weak in themselves. As Paul said, "I am well content with weaknesses . . . for when I am weak, then I am strong" (2 Corinthians 12:10). That is *spiritual strength*.

In Genesis 5:1, "This is the book of the generations of Adam." What is the book? It's the beginning of the documentation of the Bible.

That word "generations" is an interesting word. It's the Hebrew word *toledot*, and it means "generations." Whenever it is mentioned in the book of Genesis, it speaks of lineage. Go back to chapter 2 in verse 4 and I'll show you where it first occurs—after the creation account.

Moses is about to tell the creation story again, but he's not going to focus on man as the chronological last thing. He's going to focus on man as the central thing of creation. Man is not just the last act of creation, he's the central act, the *main character*. The New American Standard translation says this is the "account" or "this is *the generation* of the heavens and the earth."

We would say, this is *the story* of man. If you want to put "once upon a time," feel free because that's what it is. Moses begins to tell the history of man. And that word occurs again here in 5:1— this is "the generation of Adam."

In chapter 5, we read about the generation of Shem. Shem, the father of the Semites or the Jews. And then the generations of Abraham, then the generations of Isaac, and the generations of Jacob, and the generations of Judah will carry us to the end of Genesis.

Then in Samuel we're going to see the rise of David; and through him, Solomon; and through him, Joseph, the husband of Mary by whom is born the Christ. The Bible is going to begin a path in Genesis 5 that only one person in all of human history can walk, and that is Christ. Of all the points of Scripture you can't miss, it is who the Savior is. It tells you over and over and gets narrower and narrower. Only one Person can be that person.

My point is these people have a knowledge of who they are. They are the central characters of the narrative. They are the most important part of history. They go back to Seth "the appointed" through Noah, through Shem, through Abraham. The Jew can see who he is. They know who they are because they have a certain knowledge in essential truths. We know this because of verse 3 and following: Adam lived 130 years and became the father of a son in his own likeness, according to his image, which is named Seth. He had Seth right after Abel was killed to take the place of Abel. That was 130 years after creation.

You always think Seth's birth took place within a couple of decades. But no, the earth had grown huge because Adam had many other sons and daughters who inter-married. And you can get pretty good sized in 130 years. It tells you in verse 4, the days of Adam after he became the father of Seth were 800 years. With every one of these men, it's going to tell you how long they lived after their son was born. In verse 10, Enosh lived 815 years after he became the father of Kenan.

Verse 13, Kenan lived 840 years after he became the father of Mahalalel and so forth. No place else in the Bible does it do this. Why? Go do the math yourself. Take the birth of Seth, after him Adam's going to go 800 years and see how deep into chapter 5's genealogy you go that Adam is still around.

Would you like a conversation with Adam? Do you know how far Adam and his descendants go? Noah's father could talk with Adam! They were one generation away from an eyewitness account of the creation!!

Now, that's why this is given. The Jews among all people do not have superstition to believe in. They have an eyewitness account. And not just one of them, but nine of them are in place by the time you get to Noah. They also had twelve sons of Jacob as witnesses of their origin in Egypt and twelve tribes to spread that knowledge. What is our faith based on? "Ye shall be my witnesses." It's based upon eyewitness account of those twelve men. Here you've got the same thing: eyewitnesses and in essential areas. Do they understand God? Yes. Creation? Yes. The fall? Yes. Civilization? Yes. Who the Redeemer is? Yes, they do.

They have a knowledge of everything essential. What a woman is, what the family is? That's why I say they have a certain knowledge of essential truths. Question: Do *we* have the same thing? We have a certain knowledge passed on to us. You can get through college and if you learn all they teach, you're okay. But if you don't know God, creation, man, the fall, redemption, you're in a world of hurt.

We have a foundation of truth. I had a great-grandmother named Nette Logsdon who was born deep into the 1800s. Her father was a Miller who fought in the Civil War. I and my brother, Bobby, could sit at the feet of Nette and she would tell us about the Civil War. Can you imagine it, back in about 1960. But we would go over to her house on Summer Avenue and we would sit and listen to her and she put us in touch with who we were.

That's what this "generation" had. And they had a certain knowledge of something else. "Enoch lived sixty-five years and became the father of Methuselah" and something happened with Methuselah's birth.

"Enoch walked with God 300 years *after* he fathered Methuselah." Will becoming a father drive you to God? Yes, to God or to insanity—one of the two. What was there about Methuselah's birth that moved him to God? According to James Montgomery Boice, Methuselah means "when he dies, judgment." God gave Enoch a revelation that the world would be destroyed in one generation. The book of Jude calls Enoch a prophet who saw and proclaimed the judgment of God in the last days.

> It was also about these men that Enoch, in the
> seventh generation from Adam, prophesied,
> saying, "Behold, the Lord came with many
> thousands of His holy ones . . ." (Jude 1:14)

But the judgment promised after Methuselah would not be the final judgment but that of the flood. And that is why Enoch was taken and did not see death. He was a sign to his generation of salvation from coming judgment and the assurance of life on the other side. So does the child of God now have.

Not only do these people have an intellectual understanding of truth, they have a moral distinction. Hebrews 11:5 says, "By faith Enoch was taken up so that he would not see death; and he was not found because God took him up; for he obtained the witness that before his being taken up he was pleasing to God." This moral distinctiveness, "walking with God," was not lived in an easy day. Enoch, genealogically, is in line with Lamech in chapter 4 who boasted about his murders and his renunciation of God. And so Enoch walked with God in a difficult day indeed—the "days of Noah."

Remember Joseph? Potiphar's wife said, "Lie with me." He said, "How can I commit this great sin against God?" (see Genesis 39:9). The Bible says Jehoshaphat "took great pride in the ways of the Lord" (2 Chronicles 17:6).

These people and their descendants had a moral standard different from and higher than the world around them. Hopefully these men are starting to look familiar to you. They have truth. They have morality. They have identity. They have a certain knowledge of the coming judgment and life after death. They know who they are. They're the people of God.

We keep reading and notice what happened to every one of them. This will encourage you. At the end of verse 5, "he died"; verse 8, "he died"; verse 11, "he died"; 14, "he died"; 17, "he died." Do I need to continue? *All* of them died in faith that God would be there for them. Is that the same as us? Will your salvation let you escape physical death? Only if you're raptured.

You and I are going to die, so how long are you going to have to keep trusting and resting in God? Until you go flatline.

We're going to trust God until the end. I'm now over seventy. I discovered something about getting old: I always knew I was going to die but I thought it'd be at once. I didn't know I would die in increments. Paul said, "If our earthly tent which is our house is torn down, we have a building from God, a house not made by hands, eternal in the heavens" (2 Corinthians 5:1).

You and I are going to have to hang on and have faith that we're going to open our eyes on the other side. That's faith. "Faith is the *substance* of things hoped for, the *evidence* of things not seen" (Hebrews 11:1 KJV). Faith believes as though it has already seen what is coming.

Do we also have revelatory truth? It's called the completed Bible. What you see in Genesis 5 is the embryonic state of the Bible. The progressive revelation of God.

These people knew of what no one else had knowledge.

An amazing verse is Genesis 5:29—"Now he called his name Noah, saying, "This one will give us rest from our work and from the toil of our hands arising from the ground which the LORD has cursed." What did they name this boy? Noah means rest. They thought Noah was the seed of woman who would crush the serpent's head. This is well over a thousand years after the creation, yet what did that generation *still* know? They knew a man was coming who would save us from the curse. It's called the *protoevangelium*, "the first gospel." "The seed of woman will crush the serpent's head." They remembered that for over a thousand years! Second, He is going to give us rest from *the curse*. They believed this world was and is cursed. It's not the way it should be. The world we have is not the world we had, but the world we have is not the world we're going to have. He's going to give us rest from the curse.

Let's review:

1. These people have an identity of who they are. They are the people of God.
2. They have spiritual strength.
3. They have bold open faith in a wicked day. They call upon the name of the Lord.
4. They preserve the true knowledge of God.
5. They have a certain knowledge through eyewitness truth, just like us.
6. They walk with God. They have moral purity in a wicked day.
7. They know they're going to die.
8. They know they're going to live after death.
9. They have a book, a written revelation.
10. They have a knowledge of the coming judgment.
11. They know the delay is because of God's patience. After Methuselah dies, judgment. But Methuselah is the oldest man in the Bible.
12. Messiah will bring rest.
13. Evil wins until then.

In Genesis 7:1, God said to Noah, "You *alone* have I seen to be righteous before Me in this generation." The people of God on their own are not going to fix things. So the Church is a *lifeboat* in a dying day. We save all we can until the final judgment.

And the Church is an *influence*. We make the world a kinder, gentler place. We're light and salt. We slow down evil, but we're not going to get rid of it. How is God going to finally judge the earth? By taking us out. Just like Noah. That is why the Church acts as a "restrainer" in 2 Thessalonians 2:7–8.

Until then we keep things sane. I'm a great believer that at any time God could bring about the tribulation; all He has to do is to take us out and there's nothing to hold it back anymore. What do we do until then? We pray, we preach, we fight the good fight, we vote, we suffer, and we endure. And I hope you have discovered we're outnumbered? Yes. To be a child of the devil all you have to do is get born. To be a child of God you must be reborn.

But until the seed of woman returns, this is not our home court. We are not the home team. But if the lost are tired of evil, they can't have a prayer meeting because they don't believe in it. They can't pray. We can.

I'll tell you something else, not only can the world not pray, but they can't win. The deck is stacked. God makes the house rules. "In *Him* was life and *[His] life* was the light of men" (John 1:4). The only way you can win is to be on the winning team of God and His people. "The seed of woman shall crush the serpent's head."

Chapters 4 and 5 fascinate me. They are microcosms of the bad guys, the good guys, all guys, us guys. We don't have to stand on the curb and watch the parade of history inexplicably pass, not knowing what is coming and what is happening. We stand on a mountain and watch the parade from the beginning to the end in a glance. We see the losers. We see the winners. We see God and country.

5

Spiritual Tenacity

LUKE 18:1–8

Now He was telling them a parable to show that at all times they ought to pray and not to lose heart, saying, "In a certain city there was a judge who did not fear God and did not respect man. There was a widow in that city, and she kept coming to him, saying, 'Give me legal protection from my opponent.' For a while he was unwilling; but afterward he said to himself, 'Even though I do not fear God nor respect man, yet because this widow bothers me, I will give her legal protection, otherwise by continually coming she will wear me out.'" And the Lord said, "Hear what the unrighteous judge said; now, will not God bring about justice for His elect who cry to Him day and night, and will He delay long over them? I tell you that He will bring about justice for them

quickly. However, when the Son of Man comes,
will He find faith on the earth?"

Luke chapter 18—let me tell you what this parable is about. Luke 17 is about the Second Coming. In chapter 19, Jesus will head to the cross. Between the cross and the crown is chapter 18. What are we supposed to be doing until He returns?

Chapter 18 is about the last words of Christ. So what do you say to the people you're about to leave? Having saved us, why has God left us here? Are we simply to be calling on God to fulfill our own personal ambitions? For God to help make us rich, happy, and famous?

Chapter 18 talks about the *meantime*. In verse 1, "He told them a parable to show that at all times, they ought to pray and not to lose heart [or be discouraged]." Three things. First, you're going to need to pray. Second, you're going to need to pray continually. And third, you need not get discouraged. Discouraged means your heart gives out.

Christ is saying "I want you to be praying always and I don't want you to give up. I want you to continue. I want you to fight on." Because the fact is, the kingdom He has spoken about is not going to come about in our day. The Puritans couldn't do it, the Pilgrims couldn't do it. We can't do it. We are always going to be struggling until His return. And we are never going to be part of this world.

Peter said, "I urge you as aliens and strangers, abstain from fleshly lusts that wage war against the soul" (1 Peter 2:11). And we're *always* going to be aliens, entrusted with a divine message in a world where we are outnumbered. The message we preach is always going to be on hard, thorny ground. Satan is the father of lies, and lies do well down here. They spread very quickly.

Man is amenable to any idea absolving him from divine accountability. Ours is an out-of-place message. So don't be discouraged—pray. What do you pray for? Pray for strength to stand.

Remember the Lord's Prayer? "Thy will be done on earth as it is in heaven." Has that happened yet? No, but we're always praying "come soon." And we pray "lead us not into temptation but deliver us from evil," because we struggle in our halfway house.

In Luke 18:2, Jesus gives us a "once upon a time" kind of story. "In a certain city, there was a judge who didn't fear God and didn't respect men." You always want a judge with a sense of the divine and a sense of human dignity. This judge does not. This parable is set in a world of anarchy against God with no sense of humanity. And it looks like there is going to be *no justice*. It looks as if evil is going to win. In early Hollywood, in days of censorship, a movie could not depict sexuality or perversion; it couldn't use obscene language, and evil could not win. If a movie was taken from a book where evil won, it had to be altered and rewritten.

Sometimes one can feel we are in a scandalous movie down here. And so in Luke 18 there is a judge with whom it appears *there will be no justice*. That is the world the Church exists in today. In verse 3, there is a weak widow in the city who had been done wrong. The Old Testament is very clear God is the God of the widow and the orphan. He won't let them be harmed because a widow and an orphan have no retaliatory strength. They can't fight you. They are at the mercy of divine law to care for the widow and the orphan which is replete in the law. The widow in verse 3 persisted with the judge: "Give me legal protection from my opponent." Her rights were being violated—wrong was being done and divine law was not being instituted. This was a bad situation.

With no retaliatory ability, she kept coming to her only recourse: the law of God. Now, who are the actors here? Who is the weak widow? It's us, the Church. We are those who look for our rights to be protected by divine law. We are those who don't have any retaliatory ability so we trust upon divine justice to come to our aid. And yet there is none. The entire history of the Church has seen injustice against us. Because in a world ruled by the prince of the power of the air, who are the people who are going to get wronged the quickest? The people of God. Because they will so often be naturally despised.

Peter told the early church, "Do not be surprised at the fiery ordeal, which comes upon you for your testing, as though some strange thing is happening to you" (1 Peter 4:12). First John 3:13 says, "Do not be surprised, brethren, if the world hates you." We're not on our home court. We're not the home team. Jesus said, "In the world, you have tribulation, but take courage; I have overcome the world" (John 16:33). The apostle Paul said, "All who desire to live godly in Christ Jesus will be persecuted" (2 Timothy 3:12). "We are a fragrance of Christ to God among those who are being saved and among those who are perishing; to the one [who is perishing] an aroma from death to death, to the other (who is being saved) an aroma from life to life" (2 Corinthians 2:15–16).

"The word of the cross is foolishness to those who are perishing, but to us who are being saved it is the power of God" (1 Corinthians 1:18). Jesus said, "If they hate you, they hated Me first" (see John 15:18).

Jesus said to his brothers, who didn't believe in Him, and wanted Him to go up to Jerusalem where He could be killed, "Your time is always opportune" (John 7:6). Meaning, "You can go up to Jerusalem anytime you want, as no one is threatening you, because you tell everyone what they want to hear. *I'm* the threat." He said, "The world . . . hates Me because I testify about it, that its deeds are evil" (John 7:7). Do you remember why John the Baptist was killed? Because he told Herod who took his brother's wife, "You are wrong."

Jesus told the Twelve, "If they have called the head of the house Beelzebul, how much more will they malign the members of his household!" (Matthew 10:25). Meaning, "If they blaspheme Me, how much more they will say about you—that you are the worst thing that ever happened to this country." We are definitely in a place where there is injustice. But the Bible says, "Never take your own revenge, beloved" (Romans 12:19). Like the widow, wrong has been done to us. And like the widow, we don't begin killing people in return. So, what *do* we do? We wait on God to someday put all things right. Someday. But it doesn't come quickly. The widow in that city *kept coming* to the judge, "Give me legal protection." So do we. "Come soon, Lord Jesus." And in Luke 18:4, "For a while he was unwilling." *Justice doesn't come quickly.* So far, there has been a twenty-century respite.

For 2,000 years we have had to suffer. If you're from China or if you're from Japan, you know this. When the gospel first went to Japan, at the end of the Middle Ages, they had a rebellion against what was seen as Western thought threatening the country. The Christians were hung on crosses upside down in the surf, so when the tide came in they would all be drowned.

The United States was the anomaly of all human history. We were the one country started with the best of European Calvinistic Protestantism. The Pilgrims were the best of the English Puritans who came here to Plymouth to exercise Protestant fundamentalism. Then in the great Puritan migration in the next generation, there were 30,000 English Puritans who came to this country and formed the basis of the American worldview. And America has been a haven for 350 years.

Anybody, any place who wanted religious freedom could come here. It was written on our Mount Sinai, the Declaration of Independence, the Constitution, and Bill of Rights. You have the right to practice your religion. You can't harm someone in it, but even if you're in theological error—even if you're nuts—you can be one of our American nuts. It was called the Grand Experiment.

Well, have times changed . . . We didn't ask to be born in the greatest cultural worldview shift in history. We've been born not in the Christian era, but in the modern era. And so we are a country without God.

Mr. Rousseau of France hated the Calvinistic notion of total depravity of man. He said man is inherently good. He was your early hippie. A '60s guy long before the '60s. He felt that if you just let a child be free, their goodness will surface. You ever raised a kid? You probably became anti-Rousseauian real quick! He said if you'll just let man go and quit imposing rules on him from government and from "priestcraft" or Christianity, man will emerge and flourish.

His ideas gave rise to the French Revolution. He would be the basis of what Karl Marx would assert as a foundation for communism. He said, "The voice of the people is the voice of God." What men all intuitively want will be the voice of God. He also said some men must be forced to be free. If you don't agree then you will be killed.

This was carried on by Joseph Stalin, who said, "Death solves all problems." He killed twenty million. Chairman Mao killed twenty million. Castro, we're not sure how many he killed. We've had the guillotine. We've had the Gulag. We've had the concentration camps. We've had Siberia. Disagree and you are gone. Do you all remember a few years ago the mantra was tolerance? Those who chanted tolerance got it and they multiplied. And now they're out there and are intolerant of you.

I'll give you an example. Take a Trump sign and put it out on your lawn, see how long it stays there. Maybe you'll make it overnight. Get you a Biden sign and put it out on the lawn, it will stay there until Christ's return. Do you know why? Because removing another's sign is wrong. It is a violation of property rights, and it's a violation of coming on a man's private property. A believer in God is not going to do it because it's wrong. Absolutely.

Our country has changed. We as Christians stand against abortion because of the dignity of man in the image of God. We stand against the *enforcement* of sodomy. If I don't hire a person based on his sexual orientation, that will be regarded as a violation of his *civil rights* and you can take me to court.

I don't like the fact that you can teach in a school to my child that Sally has two daddies and homosexuality is a good thing. You can't force that in my hiring practice and my business, and you can't force that on my child. You can't punish at the university level if someone disagrees with transgenderism. It's called Cultural Marxism. Meaning, just because you are a white, male, heterosexual, cisgender, native-born you are automatically the oppressor. And if you are anything other than that you are *automatically* the oppressed and the victim. "I don't feel racist." "Well, you are a racist." "Why?" "You're a white male, heterosexual, therefore you are a racist." I don't believe that because I'm a Christian.

These ideas are not merely godless ideas people hold. They are godless ideas now being forced on us—ideas trying to become legislated. The voice of the people has become like the voice of God. The fifty-one will rule over the forty-nine, whether they like it or not. That is Orwell's *1984*.

All right, so justice won't come quickly. But what do you do? In Luke 18:5, here's what you do: you bother God. "Because this widow bothers me, I will give her legal protection." The word "bother" is the word *paraecho*. *Echo* is the Greek word that means "to hold." Like an echo, the sound doesn't fade away, it holds, it echoes. *Para* means "alongside of." *Paraecho* means to come alongside somebody and not to turn them loose.

You may remember a fellow named Samson and his Philistine wife who wouldn't let him go until he told her about a riddle. Then he had a woman named Delilah who would not turn him loose until he told her about where his strength came from. He could defeat anyone except a nagging woman. "Otherwise by continually coming she will wear me out" (v. 5), and thus, what are we supposed to do? Bother God.

This idea is taken from Isaiah. "On your walls, O Jerusalem, I've appointed watchmen." A watchman is always looking for the new day, always awaiting it. "I have appointed watchmen. All day and all night, they will never keep silent. You who *remind the LORD, take no rest* for yourselves" (62:6, emphasis added). Meaning, "I have put watchmen in your nation who are the faithful, and they are always going to look for the light. They're always going to be faithful. They're always going to keep praying." They're going to say like Jacob to the angel of Jehovah, "I will not turn you loose until you bless me." "You who remind the LORD, take no rest for yourself." Remind the Lord? I didn't know He's forgetful. We continually quote Scripture before God. As God concludes to Isaiah, "*Give Him no rest* until He establishes and makes Jerusalem a praise in the earth" (v. 7).

Christ takes up that idea in the words "pray continually and don't lose heart." Never give in. And such were the words of Christ. We are to pray and seek grace to stand and keep looking for Him to come. We are to stand firm.

A fellow named Anthony McAuliffe was general over the 101st Airborne in the city of Bastogne. It was called the Battle of the Bulge. It was the Nazis' last-ditch push to save themselves. They massed all their army and overran us, and the 101st was trapped in Bastogne. They were short of food, short of ammunition—it looked like obliteration. A German commander sent them an invitation to surrender or to be obliterated. Anthony McAuliffe sent back one word, "Nuts." A response that became enshrined in American history.

In the same way we endure as long as we ought.

They said to Paul, "Don't go to Jerusalem." Paul said, "My brethren, why are you breaking my heart? I am ready not only to suffer but also to die for the name of the Lord Jesus. I count my life to be of no account that I might finish my course that I received from the Lord Jesus to testify solemnly of the grace of God" (see Acts 20). You know what that means? "Nuts." The pattern for Paul's devotion was set in an earlier day.

Ruth was told by Naomi, "I can't promise you anything, I can't give you a husband, I can't have more kids, I'm going to go back a widow, you're going to go back a widow also." And Ruth said, "Wherever you go there I will go. Where you lie down I'll lie down, where you die I'll die, where you're buried I'm buried, and your people will be my people, your God my God" (see Ruth 1:15–17). Realizing she could not be deterred, they left together. Ruth just said, "Nuts." So with us, no matter how tough it gets, you say, "Nuts. I'm going to fight through."

You and I are Normandy. In a wicked world the coming of Christ was the landed invasion of planet earth. Now we come ashore and we're pressing toward Berlin. We're living now for what's going to happen in future days. So we fight on. We're going to conquer. What's God doing right now? He is gathering out a people and He will most assuredly come for us.

But we are told, "Hear what the unrighteous judge said. Will not God bring about justice for His elect?" The thought is, if a *godless* judge will bring about justice because he is continually sought, will not *a just God* bring justice for his elect who cry to Him night and day? Will He not set things right? Will He not finally punish evil?

In Luke 18:8, "He *will* bring about justice for them quickly." That word "quickly" doesn't mean Christ will rise and then one week later the Second Coming will happen. The word "quickly" is used in Revelation 1:1, ". . . the things which must quickly take place." It means when He's done with what He's doing, He'll be back. The Lord will not tarry.

Until that time, pray always. Do not give up. A widow beseeches; she gets justice. How much more will we pray and get justice once Jesus has gathered His elect.

Back to Luke 18:8, Christ ends this text in a question. "But when the Son of Man comes" (note the word "when," as opposed to the word "if"), "will He find faith on the earth?" I'll be faithful, how about you? "Are you going to be faithful when I show up?" or "don't worry about me, worry about you. Am I going to find *the faith*?" Will the Church hold fast to the Word of God during this age before His returning in justice?

In 1929, Princeton seminary abandoned the doctrine of inerrancy and that's when my seminary, Dallas Seminary, started. As a matter of fact, of all the Ivy League colleges, only one, Cornell, was *not* begun by Christians to train ministers. Dartmouth was called Moore's Indian Training School to train Indians converted in the First Awakening. Those early Christian institutions have abandoned their position.

"Will He find faith?" Who do you think has been more faithful? God to His people? Or the Church to His Word? It has been God to His people, not the Church to His Word. I and my church are known as fundamental. We have a biblical morality and see the sovereignty of God in all things and seek to take every thought captive to the obedience of Christ. But we are a splinter group. We are in a shrinking minority. What happened to the Church? Do you know what the Christian manifesto is?

The Communist Manifesto was Karl Marx setting forth what he believed in a declaration, as he didn't feel communists should be underground. They were to be out there in your face. That was a Communist Manifesto.

The Christian manifesto is ten points:

1. We believe in an infinite personal God who is Trinity.
2. We believe He is the creator of all and He is sovereign over all things.
3. We believe He is intuitively discovered. All men know He is there. You are not born an atheist. You are born with an awareness that there's someone above you.

4. We believe man has infinite eternal dignity as in the image of God. Man, woman, child, and the child in the womb.

5. Man is fallen. He is dead. He cannot know God on his own.

6. God has made Himself known in the Bible.

7. There is *absolute* right and *absolute* wrong. The voice of the people is not the voice of God. The Word of God is the voice of God to His people and all men.

8. God has sent His Son to die for man's sins and grant him eternal life.

9. Christ is going to return.

10. He is going to judge the living and the dead.

That is called a Christian manifesto. Undeniable truths, much like the Apostles' Creed.

Well, can I tell you what this world we are presently in has done for me? These last few years the world has lost its allure to me. I don't feel quite the tug to be worldly anymore. We can see it for what it is a little more clearly—the media, politics, the arts, sports, the universities, the schools. This world has made me more content with the simple knowledge of salvation.

Have you heard of David Livingstone? An English missionary in the 1800s to Africa—explorer, doctor, missionary. England lost touch with him. H. M. Stanley went over to find him. He found him with malaria and wanted to bring him home. Livingstone said to Stanley, "I'm not going anywhere. This is where I want to be." At the end of his life, they found him dead beside his bed on his knees praying for Africa. The natives took his body and walked to the coast to send it back to England where he was buried at Westminster Abbey. But the Africans kept his heart and they buried it in Tanganyika. That was where his heart was. That's what you call being faithful until the end.

These were among the last words spoken by Jesus before He entered Jerusalem to die. These are our working orders. Stand firm . . . pray . . . preach the Word . . . and wait. And await the question, "When the Son of Man comes, will He find faith on the earth?"

Such is the responsibility of the Church to God and country.

6

Social Reconciliation

JOHN 13:35

"By this all men will know that you are My
disciples, if you have love for one another."

Philemon. Philemon is an odd little book. We call it the book of Philemon, but it's really just a letter, and it's not really a letter; it's a note. Actually, it's really Colossians 5. Paul from prison sent the letter of Colossians in the hand of Tychicus, and he put in a little note.

He said, "I want you to give this to the man that the Colossian church meets in his home. His name is Philemon. The pastor's name is Archippus. That's his son. The lady who is the queen of the church, that's Philemon's wife, Apphia. You give him this because somebody is going with you that's one of their number that used not to be. His name is Onesimus and he's a runaway slave who stole from him before he ran away. And he's gotten saved" (see Philemon 1:1–16).

How would you like to be in jail with the apostle Paul?

But Paul bloomed where he was planted. He sent a letter back, a little note about this fellow named Onesimus whom he called "my child whom I have begotten in my imprisonment" (v. 10). Now, here's why Philemon is an interesting book. It's the last book of the Pauline canon. There are thirteen books. The first is Romans that sits at the head of the table.

After the book of Acts, we don't see historically what Paul did. He wrote 1 Timothy, Titus, and then finished up with 2 Timothy. The pastoral epistles are his last works. Philemon is put last in those thirteen works, and it's out of place. It should be right there with Colossians as a prison epistle, but it's put last because it's the proper bookend. It's the bow on your New Testament.

If Romans is true, and in Christ you are forgiven, made a child of God, your name written in the heavenlies, and you are loved with everlasting love. If you have been made complete in Christ, adopted into His family, reconciled to God, does that then change how I see a Christian brother? Yes, it does. No matter what he used to be. "Old things passed away; behold, new things have come" (2 Corinthians 5:17).

What if he is on a totally different socioeconomic, racial, educational, sociological place in life? Do I go against all conventions and see him as my brother? Yes, I do. That is why if Romans is true, you must have a Philemon. If Romans is true, you could almost see the devil's advocate saying, "You're saying to me that all these things are true if you are in Christ?" "Right."

"Then what if a guy steals from you, is in jail, gets led to Christ, and comes back, and you have a right within Roman custom to put him to death as a runaway slave who stole from you. You now have to regard him as brother?" What's the answer? *Yes*, you do. Yes. If Romans is true, you must have a Philemon. And if Philemon is true, we have found the golden fleece. We have found (are you ready?) "social justice." We found it. We have found racial reconciliation; we have found the garden of Eden if this is true.

Francis Schaeffer once said about communism that it was a Christian heresy, and he was right. It is trying to bring equality without God. "You will treat each other as equals or I'll kill you." That's communism. It doesn't work well. It's a Christian heresy. Only through Romans can you have a Philemon.

In verse 1, "Paul, a prisoner of Christ Jesus." This was his first Roman imprisonment, where he wrote Ephesians, Philippians, Colossians, and Philemon. He was a prisoner of Christ Jesus. And here was Philemon, also a beloved brother and a fellow worker. This was a good man.

In verse 2, his family were leaders in the Colossian church. "Apphia, our sister," that's Philemon's wife. "Archippus, our fellow soldier" (he's also mentioned in Colossians 4) is believed to have been Philemon's son who was pastor of the church.

But the letter is written "to the church in your house" because the lesson he would teach was not just for Philemon. If it's true for Philemon, it is a lesson for *all* of the Church, for all of history. If you ask a non-Christian about why he isn't a Christian and he gives a pragmatic reason, probably this is what he has seen—an inconsistency between belief and behavior.

The Jim Crow laws. How could those exist in a Christian country where a man can be my brother in Christ, but he can't drink from my water fountain or attend my church? How do you arrive at that? I've been to old churches in South Carolina where they have the floor seating, and then they have the balcony for black Christians.

I am told the African Methodist Episcopal Church started because a church was going to put new tiles in the pulpit area and a group of black Christians paid for some. They came up on the pulpit area to pray over them. One of the workers in the church told them to get out of there, they had no place in that area.

They said, "We're members." He said, "Well, you got to find your place," and he ran them off. It so insulted them they left and that was what began the AME church. That's sad. And it's unbiblical that black Christians were forced to that decision. Paul writes to this good man and to this good family, for all the church to hear.

In verses 4 and 5, Paul was thankful: "I thank my God always, making mention of you in my prayers, because I hear of your love and of the faith which you have toward the Lord Jesus." How do you hear of a man's love and faith? You can't see faith, but you can see what faith produces. "I hear of the faith which you have toward Christ." People talk about the visible evidence of Christian faith.

In verse 6, the evidence of his faith is about to go deeper than it has ever gone before. Let me ask you, can we all have a relationship with God, and yet, can God take us to places in our Christian life where Christian obedience is going to penetrate to a depth it has never been? It happens all the time.

When somebody in a school mistreats your child, you go to a place you have never been before. Or when a doctor gives you an x-ray and then tells you with a grim face to have a seat. Or one gets married and all of a sudden biblical obedience goes to a place it has never been before.

Well, this is about to happen in Philemon's life. He has been loving all his life but he's about to have someone in his life he's never had to love before. In verse 6, "And I pray that the fellowship of your faith." Now this is a one-time mentioning of a phrase once mentioned by Paul. Have you ever heard of the term *koinonia*? *Koinonia* means commonality or communion. We say in the Apostles' Creed, "I believe in the holy Catholic church," meaning the universal church, "and in the communion of the saints," the local church—it has a communion, a fellowship.

You may have a Bible that says "the sharing of your faith." That doesn't mean witnessing; it means how you relate to other Christians. The communion or the fellowship or the sharing of your faith. Have you ever seen those verses in the book of Acts where they took their meals together with sincerity and gladness of heart. No one regarding anything as belonging to them, sharing with any who might have need (see 2:44–47). That's called the koinonia of your faith, the sharing of your faith, the living out of your faith.

Are these your brothers? Your equals? Yes. Is God our Father? Yes. Then there's a way you're going to relate to each other. A communion. "I pray that the fellowship of your faith, may become effective" (Philemon 1:6). Now, this word "effective" is a combination of two words: *ergos*, meaning "work"; then "to work at." What word do we get? *energos*, energy. "I pray that the fellowship of your faith *can be at work* through the knowledge of every good thing that is in you for Christ's sake."

The reason a Christian has an effective faith is through the "knowledge of the good things" God has done for him. I love you when I see you. Why? Because I have a knowledge of the good things Christ has done in me. I know you are loved by God, you are a child of God, you're forgiven by God, you're in progress by God of shaping, that you're going to be with me forever in heaven.

Because of my knowledge of the good things in you for Christ's sake, the communion of our faith is effective.

In a sense, the whole book turns on this verse because he's about to be told he's got to love someone who is difficult to love. The reason he's going to love him is because of what God has done for that man. When I was saved in 1972, the biggest change I saw was when I went down into the dorm cafeteria the next day. Something changed in how I saw people. There were hippies, there were rednecks, there were music majors, and athletes, but all were seen as priceless treasures.

It was because I saw men like God sees them. I didn't try to seek change but something changed. In verse 7, Paul states that Philemon had a history of being a loving person. "I have come to have much joy and comfort in your love because the hearts of the saints have been refreshed through you."

That's past tense. People in past days said, "Philemon, you're a delight. You're a joy to us." Often in the ministry you can be discouraged until you get around people you have "come to have much joy and comfort in their love." You see how they're growing and you just say, "Man, it's worth it. It really is." Paul says to Philemon, "You've given me a lot of delight, but God's not through with you. We're about to put you to the acid test." Can you love a man completely because of who he has become in Christ?

It goes like this. "We recognize no one according to the flesh; even though we have known Christ according to the flesh, yet now we know Him in this way no longer" (2 Corinthians 5:16). We used to have a pagan notion of Christ, but it's changed. That's the same way we see people. We regard no man according to his flesh, his race, his education, his social status, his handicap, his whatever. We don't see it anymore. "If anyone is in Christ, he is a new creature" (2 Corinthians 5:17).

The context is not talking about how we see ourselves. The context is how I see you. I don't see Christ the same as I used to. I don't see His people the same as I used to. "Old things passed away. New things have come." That verse is not merely about the reconciliation of the believer to God. It's about the reconciliation of the believer to others. There *is* social justice found in the Christian church. This is the golden fleece we've all been looking for. Here it is. Finally, we found it. "Beat your swords into plowshares . . . and study war no more."

Well in verse 8 we're about to dig deep. We move now from the memories of verse 7 to verse 8. "Though, I have enough confidence in Christ to order you to do what is proper," meaning, "I could order you as an apostle to do something, but I'm not going to do it." And it's because of verse 9. It would be an insult to Christ. "For love's sake,

I rather appeal to you—since I am such a person as Paul—the aged and now a prisoner of Christ Jesus." He says, "I'm in jail, and I'm in jail because of you, because of preaching the gospel to you. In light of my sufferings, I'm going to ask you to do something not because you have to, but because you want to. Because you love me."

What Paul is going to ask Philemon to do is verse 10, "I appeal to you for my child." If Onesimus is Paul's child, who is he to Philemon? His brother. I'm asking you to do something because of who I am and because of who this man is. "I appeal to you for my child, Onesimus, whom I have begotten in my imprisonment." Meaning, I was the obstetrician and I brought this man to birth. I delivered him. Now what's interesting, the word *Onesimus* means "useful" in Greek. In verse 11, he formerly was "useless," or "worthless."

He was useless. He was a thief, a runaway. He ran away to Rome where he could get lost but he was of the elect of God and couldn't run away. God stuck him in jail with the apostle Paul—a captive audience. In verse 11, he was useless, but now is useful. You know what we would say? He is now Onesimus. He's useful. This is a picture of us and God. When we were non-Christians we were—and I quote Titus 1:16—"worthless for any good deed." But now we have become useful or worthy. God has done a work in us. In verse 12, "I have sent him back to you in person . . . sending my very heart." I want to stop here just a second.

Onesimus, we're going to find out later, stole from Philemon. I'm sure Philemon treated him well. It's to the Colossian church Paul said, "and masters, grant to your slaves justice and fairness, knowing that you too have a Master in heaven" (Colossians 4:1). I'm sure he was very good to this slave. But Onesimus stole from Philemon and he ran away. "I am sending him back to you." You know why? Because even though he became a Christian and was now serving God and helping Paul, to serve God well, he had to clear his conscience. We may have done some things that wronged people and we can't speak boldly until we get them cleared. "The righteous are as bold as lions, but the wicked flee when no one is pursuing." When your conscience isn't strong, you don't have confidence.

After I was saved, I remember having to go back to my old quarterback coach. He would curse me till a fly would not light on me and I would curse him back. Then I was saved and I began sharing my testimony. I began wondering, what would I do if that coach walked in the back of the church? Could I talk to him? His last job when he retired from coaching was to manage the University of North Texas basketball arena. I said, "God, if I ever run into him, I'll do what I have to."

I went to a game and took my son, Ben, and we walked in and I looked up and there he was. I thought, *Dang! Me and my prayers.* I said, "Ben, go in and sit down. I'll be in directly." I said, "Coach, those were dark days in my life. I was a typical rebellious nineteen-year-old. I need to ask your forgiveness." He said, "Well, Tommy, I ought to be asking you the same thing."

You know what? We got straight. I was free to witness and did. It's interesting, even though Onesimus was in the ministry with Paul, Paul sent him back to be reconciled. But Paul says to the offended Philemon, "I'm sending him back to you in person and I'm sending my very heart." You may remember Jacob had a couple of sons, Joseph and Benjamin, who were sons of his old age because they took care of him. That is what Onesimus was to the apostle Paul—his Joseph, his Benjamin. "As I'm an old man in prison, this man takes care of me. I'm sending to you my heart."

That's what discipleship is: I'm sending you my heart. In verse 13, "whom I wished to keep with me, so that on your behalf he might minister to me." Meaning, "I don't have the right to ask him to serve if you don't give the okay. I'm not going to force my will upon you and say because I'm an apostle, you have to let this man work with me." No, that's an insult to the grace of God. In verse 14, "without your consent I did not want to do anything, so that your goodness would not be by compulsion but of your own free will."

I will not insult the grace of God by making you do what grace should impel you. Such is an insult to Christ. It's an insult to the gospel and it's an insult to me, and to you.

In verses 15 and 16, Paul gives a number of reasons as to why Onesimus should be forgiven. As I show these to you, you're going to start thinking to yourself, *Those sound familiar to what God has done for all of us through Christ.*

Paul is a great picture of Christ.

We are a great picture of *Philemon.*

Treating the body of Christ is like *Onesimus.* And that is difficult for us in many ways.

Have you ever heard the old adage, "To live above with saints we love, oh, that will be glory. To live below with those we know, well, that's a different story"? Sometimes it's hard to love humans, or as the great apostle Lucy said in *Peanuts*, "I love the world. It's just people that I hate."

The mission's director in our church once said he was going to begin a church called No People Bible. He just wouldn't have to mess with people. That's what it was like ministering during COVID. No humans!

You may have heard of the guy who was marooned at sea, and when they found him they saw three little huts on the beach. They said of the first hut, "What was this?" "That's where I live." Of the second hut, "What was this?" "I always missed church so I had to build me a church." Of the third hut, "What was this?" "Well, I left the first church and I went over to this one." It's called the Protestant church growth method.

Over verses 15 and 16, write the word *adoption*. "Perhaps he was for this reason separated from you for a while, that you would have him back forever." Paul said maybe this bad thing happened to you, a runaway thieving slave, so there would be a higher good. Lost for a while to have him back forever. Maybe this hardship happened to him for God to bring him to the end of his rope so he could be converted.

Is there ever a time we have to apply that? Where like Joseph you say, "You meant it for evil, but God meant it for good." Sometimes you can see the will of God clearer when you look behind and see what He's done.

Most of us have heard of Augustine. Augustine was a college professor, philosopher, and a sex addict who already had a son born out of wedlock. He ran away from North Africa to Rome where there were no holds barred. His mother was named Monica and she prayed for him and while she was on her knees praying, the little booger snuck out and went away and immersed himself in sin. Through that, however, he hit the bottom and was converted and became Saint Augustine.

Sometimes God has to separate someone to work in their lives. In verse 16, to have Onesimus back "no longer as a slave, but more than a slave, a beloved brother." Meaning, "If he is my child in the faith, he is your brother, because I led you both to Christ. I want you to see him as a brother."

But note he says, in verse 16, "how much more to you, both *in the flesh* and *in the Lord*." This is the phrase that rocks me. I'll tell you why. What that means is, you can't merely look at him and call him a brother "*in the Lord*." He's a brother "*in the flesh*." What does this mean? Would you agree sometimes it's easy to call a Christian a spiritual brother, but not let him sit at the table with you? For one to be a brother "in the Lord" but not socially, or "in the flesh."

In my church is a very successful internist from India named Manny. He told me his grandfather was one of the leaders of Indian Methodism. He was a leader because when he became a Christian he was converted out of Hinduism. If you know anything about Hinduism, there is a certain group of people in the Hindu caste system on the bottom called the "Untouchables." They are seen to be suffering for their sins in a past life as they had bad "karma," or their sin from a previous life was being recompensed on them. There are mothers who will break the bones of their Untouchable children so they can suffer more to get out of what they deserve in the next life.

Reincarnation has held that country in bondage and in ignorance. But Manny's grandfather trusted Christ and he recognized if he was really a Christian, he could not be a Christian merely academically and theologically, it had to show up both "in the flesh and in the Lord." If an Untouchable has trusted in Christ, then he is my brother. And if he is my brother, he is my brother in the Lord *and* in the flesh.

Now, what do you do if you're in an Indian church, and the Untouchables can come and sit, but they can't take communion because they have to eat with you? Manny's grandfather said, "No." Though Hinduism has been around since 3000 BC, he said, "No." And that tradition fell in the light of Christ. Manny told me, "That's the way that in India you can tell if an Indian Christian is the real thing. He'll do away with over five millennia of error simply by a moment's faith in Christ." He is your brother in the flesh and in the Lord.

Did you ever see the movie *Remember the Titans* with Denzel Washington? A true story set in Alexandria, Virginia. Busing brought blacks and whites together, but was hard on a black kid because he had to leave what he was to come to a white school. It was tough on everybody. But in Virginia the blacks and whites were together on a football team— the ultimate team sport. The white coach who was the head coach became the assistant, and a black coach took over by rule of the city council. There were hard feelings. They took these two groups of kids to two-a-day workouts away from Alexandria.

They tried to bring them together and they did so by a white defensive end, and a black defensive end who were team leaders. They brought the team together and said, "We've got to play as a team," and during two-a-day workouts, they rallied to each other's defense. They had great two-a-day workouts filled with joyful unity *until* they got on the bus and came back home. They now had to go among their peers, and this is in Virginia. This is the former slave state. Once they got within the scrutiny of their white and black colleagues, all of their commitment went out the door.

They were willing to be unified theoretically but not socially. "It's good that we say that we're equals, but we're talking here about the lunchroom and we don't do that." The two kids who were the two captains called the team together in a gym, and they said, "We can't just call ourselves unified when we're by ourselves. We've got to do this in public." And the white kids learned how to dance like black kids (no small thing). They transformed the school.

You can't just say, "We're equals in Christ." You've got to say, "This is my brother." "He's an Untouchable." "This is my brother." "He's the thief." "This is my brother." We don't normally do things like that. Not in this life we don't. But this is the Church. We're ruled by King Jesus. We have *social justice*. We don't just have it in doctrine, we have it here. We're Christians. You see why I say that if you're going to have a Romans, you've got to have a Philemon. It can't be theoretical. We've got to see it done. If there is no Philemon, throw away Romans. It doesn't work. This is *really* the solution to life—Christ. Non-Christians are looking for Philemon.

A good example was when Paul was converted on the Damascus Road and God told a Christian brother named Ananias, "There's a man at the house of Judas on the street called Straight and he's praying. His name is Saul." Ananias said, "Excuse me. Could I have a word? Wasn't this the guy coming up here to beat us?" God said, "Yes, he's a chosen vessel and he's going to be the greatest missionary who ever lived." Ananias went to Paul and immediately said, "*Brother* Saul, God has appeared to you and appointed to you to know His will" (see Acts 9:1–17). It took Ananias one second. You're my brother if you're God's child. That is original Christianity.

Because of adoption, we love them no matter who that person is. Over verse 17, write down the word *imputation*. If you regard me a partner, an equal, accept him as you would me. "See him like you see me. "If any man is in Christ, he's a new creation." I see the man as I see Christ. That's too good to be true. It's New Testament. Verse 18 is "imputed demerit." "If he's wronged you in any way or owes you anything, I'll pay it. Charge that to my account." Does that sound like somebody you know? It sounds like Jesus. "I'm going to give to him My righteousness and I will take his sin."

Just like us and Christ. Adoption and imputation look familiar. It is. It is a crayon drawing pointing to a heavenly reality. I can touch this and see it and understand it. If you'll notice in verse 19, there is forgiveness. "I, Paul, I'm writing this with my own hand." Paul usually didn't write his own letters, he dictated them. But Paul says, "Give me the pen." He writes with his big scrawl. He signs it.

"This is my authority and I'm saying to you, I will repay it. Not to mention to you that you owe to me *even your own life* as well" (see v. 19). There is forgiveness. "Philemon, you can forgive Onesimus because you owe your life to Christ. God forgave you. If God has forgiven you, you can forgive him." Remember Jesus's story in Matthew 18 about the slave who owed $18 million in silver and he was forgiven.

Another owed him eighteen bucks and he choked him. His master came back and said, "Toss him in prison." So it shall be for you if you do not forgive those who harm you.

How can I say I have known the forgiveness of an infinite debt and I can't forgive another? If he has sinned against me, he is like me. If he has sinned against you, he is like you. They are sinners and we are sinners. Paul goes on to say, in verse 20, "Yes, brother, let me benefit from you in the Lord; refresh my heart in Christ." When you get among people where there is the communion of the saints, it lifts your heart in refreshment.

You ever been in a church rent by anger and unforgiveness? It's depleting to your soul. Proverbs 25:25 says, "Like cold water to a weary soul, so is good news from a distant land." When you walk in a place where there is love, you think "that's the real deal." I spoke one time at a Fellowship of Christian Athletes college retreat and I taught Philippians 2:6–7, "Although [Christ] existed in the form of God, He didn't regard equality with God a thing to be grasped, but emptied Himself, taking the form of a bondservant, and being made in the likeness of men."

I said to these college athletes, "If Jesus Christ can die for us, what can you do for your brother?" I made them write it down. "If Jesus Christ could give His life for me, I can . . ." And you had to write down something you were going to do for three days. "If He can wash men's feet, I can _____ men's _____."

One man put, "I can stand for them in the lunch line and bring them their lunch." One twenty-year-old said, "I can go get Tommy Nelson coffee at 6:00 in the morning." Amen!

Another said, "I can go sweep out their room." Another, "I can carry their luggage." We all had to make a commitment. If Jesus could do this for us, we can do this for others. For three days, the most arrogant men on planet Earth—college athletes—had to serve each other.

At the end of that time, we were in the lunchroom and this woman came up to me and said, "Who are these men? I've never seen such godly men." I said, "These are possibly the most arrogant human beings in the state of Texas." She thought it was a group of Benedictine monks—large, hairy Benedictine monks. "No, these are simply Christians who have committed to live out their faith for seventy-two hours." I had men say to me it was the greatest three days of their lives. One said, "I no longer had to live up to anything. I could just be a servant." He said, "This is my natural habitat."

In verse 21, it reads, "Having confidence in your obedience, I write to you, since I know that you will do even more than what I say." Law does all it must; grace does all it can. That is the grace of God. In verse 22, "At the same time also prepare me a lodging, for I hope that through your prayers I'll be given to you." He simply says to Philemon, "I'm going to return." There's going to be a second coming of the apostle Paul. "I came to you first preaching grace and I am about to return and it's for judgment. I want to see if you have lived out the life that you said you would."

Does that sound familiar? You and I will be called to account as good stewards. Let me just close with this idea. America was blessed because as the rationalistic Enlightenment was setting into Europe, out of which would come the most heinous ideologies in history. That of communism, fascism, theological liberalism, atheism, existentialism, and as these ideas would spread into Cuba and China and South East Asia and Russia, the last words of George Washington ring true, "Beware of Europe." Because in Europe God was being set aside and man exalted.

It is speculated the only reason the French Revolution didn't come to England was because of the English revivals and the preaching of John Wesley. Europe was literally beginning to go up in flames. At the same time America was having its constitutional convention.

As Europe was beginning to incinerate, God took the best of all Protestant Christian theology and let it wash up on our shores. It was called the Puritan migration when 30,000 Puritans showed up in America. The American worldview became the Judeo-Christian idea. America began with what no other country had. We had a Mount Sinai-like document reflecting the sovereignty of God. It is called the American Constitution.

We had checks and balances because we were Calvinistic oriented and we didn't trust man to always do justly. Absolute power corrupts absolutely. We believed that, so we had checks and balances. It was the greatest government in history. The greatest government is to have a God who speaks who becomes a man and governs you, but until Christ is on the ballot, the best we can do is to take a reflection of the Bible, put it in a document by which kings must put their hand down and swear by God to keep. If they don't, we can remove them. That's the greatest government of all time until Christ comes. I think the reason God let us come here is so when it all hit the fan in Europe, people had to get out of there. Guess where they came? They came to a land where there was a Statue of Liberty at its threshold.

We said, "Bring to me your wretched huddled masses." We have an inalienable right from nature's God. And we weren't thinking of Allah or a pantheistic force. It was the God of the Bible. When you come here, we have a Bill of Rights, and you have freedom of speech, the right to assemble, to bear arms, and freedom to worship. These are yours along with a trial by a jury of your peers. It's inalienable. No one can deny us these rights.

And that's why everyone lined up to get in. But when a people reject God, that will be a particular nation in harm's way. A nation under constant threat. Israel. But what nation opened and said to the Jew "come over" and they came? God has used *America* for marvelous things indeed.

But we have an Achilles' heel in our nation; we have had it since the first slave ship came. Since the Civil War, since Jim Crow, since Rodney King. It is called racism. It's a sin in man. When man wants to be like God and have nobody unlike him, there is sin. Racism. Our country has always struggled with it because we're a multi-racial country—a multi-racial group of sinners.

We're not a melting pot as much as a mosaic. You can say a Frenchman, and you get a visual idea. You say an Englishman, you get an idea. Scot, Irishman, African, Asian. An American? You can't get one picture. We're all things. We're a nation of immigrants. Thus, a totally rational person would say, "That's a marvelous place where all these people can come. That's wonderful. How precious."

But the totally rational would also say, "That's going to be a great nation. However, they're going to have a problem because if anybody can come, they're going to have to live together in peace. But if there's anything we know about humans, they can't do that. Men are natural-born racists." They have towers of Babel and confusion. They can't do it. America is a skeleton of what unity should be but without the heart to enliven it.

We have coded into us as Americans a rock in our shoe. We can never get too cocky and too impressed with ourselves. Because we can punish racism in Germany but we can't fix it here. It reminds us that the only way you can have diversity and unity is with the Trinity—and with the atonement by Christ for all men by which through grace they are made brothers. It's as if God has rigged it: we're never going to have complete peace in this country or in this world.

Is racism wrong? Yes. Is rioting wrong? Yes, both occasions. White guys are wrong being racist; black guys are wrong rioting and burning everything. The pendulum swings. Satan takes it both ways. The only way to fix it is to say all men have dignity and to seek absolute biblically informed justice.

Christ is our only means of getting this together. That's why this book is so essential. Is there a place in our country that's got it right? Yes. The Church. We are the people who become the light of the world and the salt of the earth. Everything would be great if we would just become what we ought and if all would become like us.

The Christian Church (the Body of Christ) has the only true means of social justice. It alone understands "social." It alone has a standard for justice. And the classic book of social justice is Philemon. Each and every maxim of conduct is personified in the absolute standard of Jesus. He is our point of reference as to how we treat people.

But the sad thing is Christians can fail to live this out. And so we pray "that the fellowship of your faith may become effective through the knowledge of every good thing that is in you for Christ's sake" (v. 6).

Where there is salvation by grace there must necessarily be unity. Where there is a Romans, there must be a Philemon.

There is God. And then there is country.

7

Continental Collapse

JUDGES 8:22

Then the men of Israel said to Gideon, "Rule over us, both you and your son, your son's son as well, for you have saved us from the hand of Midian!"

Let's take a look at Judges 8:22 and let's go all the way through chapter 9. Let me begin with just a statement: there are two things you're not supposed to speak of in polite company—politics and religion. The reason is because, number one, they're both very volatile. Religion involves the most important area of thought and that is how you relate to the eternal God which determines all of your actions. It's been said if you want to study theology and ideas, just study history. History is the working out of ideas. Politics also is volatile. It involves who's going to rule us. Who's going to get their hands on our money, and who's going to curtail our freedoms. Or declare what the freedoms will be. What will we do with bad guys and good guys, and do we know who the bad guys and good guys are? The politicians are going to get a hold of my kids, and so this goes deep.

And number two, these areas of politics and religion, are very personal. That is why we debate them so much. These areas go very deep. They are the warp and the woof of who we are. When someone would challenge our beliefs in God and in politics, my father would say, "you got me by the short hairs." I don't know what that meant, but when he would grab me, I knew what that meant. These are all personal opinions unless you have a Bible. Unless you have the Word of God which majors in these areas. The Bible does not waste your time. It deals with religion. On how you approach God, and who God is. Then it addresses how this heavenly King is to rule you.

As a matter of fact, the chief character in the Bible combines the office of the priest and king in one Person: Jesus. He is the nail-pierced Priest who determines religion. He is the exalted King. His kingdom comes, and His will be done on earth as it is in heaven. All of the Bible deals with priests and kings. With religion and with politics. The reason I say this is because in Judges 6–9, those chapters are a watershed in Israel's history. They deal with the person of Gideon, and Gideon's son, Abimelech. In Judges 1–5, we have stellar judges—Othniel, Ehud, Deborah. They're flawless.

Then on the other side of Gideon we see a decline. We have Jephthah who was a robber, and we have Samson who had some struggles with the ladies. Have you ever noticed when the nation goes down, its heroes go down? In this case their politicians go downward. Now, Gideon started off really well. He was a great military man until he had to rule. There he started taking many wives, and we're going to see seventy kids come from them.

Then we're going to see what comes from them. We're going to see a particular boy who, if you preach on him, he can only be called "the man who would be king." Abi Melech, "My father is king." Abimelech. He's only going to rule for three years. He's not going to make it one term, and he will commit perhaps the greatest atrocity in the history of Israel to this point. We're going to see who puts him there, why they put him there, and what happens to a country that puts a man in rule simply because there are personal agendas you like about them. "A divine decision is in the lips of a king; his mouth should not err in judgment" (Proverbs 16:10). He is to articulate the will of God.

With that in mind, this fellow, Abimelech, is going to begin a civil war. He's going to kill people. He's going to kill those who followed him, until he's killed in a very ignominious way. He is the classic in juxtaposition to the coming kings of what we do not want. In Judges 8:22, Gideon has just conquered the oppressors of Israel, the Midianites.

He's got a lamp inside a clay jar, and he's got a trumpet. He's victorious by the grace of God. "Then the men of Israel said to Gideon, 'Rule over us, both you and your son, also your son's sons.'" What were they asking for? They were asking for a dynasty. This is long before Saul and the request, "Give us a king like the Gentiles." This is the first man who would be king. The nation was inviting him to establish the Gideon monarchy. The reason is in verse 22, "for you have delivered us from the hand of Midian."

In other words, "You're a great military leader to fight our battles. We want government to save us. We want government to preserve us," and Gideon saw it. He said in verse 23, "'I will not rule over you, nor shall my son rule over you. [Yahweh] shall rule over you.'" He said, "Boys, you don't need a politician, and you don't need a king. You need God—God will rule you." "It's to the glory of God to conceal a matter, to the glory of kings to search it out" (Proverbs 25:2).

What is the will of God? That's what a king should seek.

Gideon said in verse 24, "'I would request of you, that each of you give me an earring from his plunder. (For they had gold earrings because they were Ishmaelites," who were Bedouins.) They collected the pillage of war from the Midianites. And Gideon is going to do what you call a compromise. How much better it would've been if Gideon said, "We're going back to the law and the testimony."

At this time the tabernacle was at Shiloh. Gideon could have said, "We will have the law of God taught to us and we will go back. We will not be progressive and go on, we will reform and we will go back." How much better it would have been had he done this, but he didn't. With an ignorant and disobedient generation, Gideon made a compromise. He sought to make God user-friendly. He came down to the level of the people. He didn't reform; he became progressive.

This is what I felt back in the '80s and '90s when I saw the emergent church. When we started having sermonettes for Christianettes and dumbing down everything. No longer teaching Bible exposition, no longer teaching theology, no longer calling to a moral standard. It became how God can make you happy and healthy and successful. We're paying for it. You don't compromise the Bible because of your crowd. You come up where the Bible is. You don't go where they are.

The men of Israel said in verses 25–26, "'We will surely give them.' So they spread out a garment and every one of them threw an earring there from his spoil. The weight of the gold earrings he requested was 1,700 shekels of gold." That's forty-two pounds of gold. "Besides the crescent ornaments and the pendants, and the purple robes which were on the kings of Midian, and besides the neck bands that were on their camels' necks." Incidentally, do you remember another occasion where a spiritual leader said, "Give me all of your gold"? And he made it into something called a golden calf, and the nation sat down to eat and drink, and they rose up to play or commit immorality. Because you can't get a moral absolute from an animal, alive or golden.

In verse 27, Gideon made it into an ephod. An ephod is not a golden calf. He improved on that. It's a religious article. The high priest, when he came into the presence of God, would have a robe and he would have a tunic. On the outside of it he would have a workman's apron or an ephod. It had shoulder straps. On the breastplate he had twelve stones to represent the twelve tribes of Israel. On the shoulders were two onyx stones, on which were inscribed six tribes and six tribes. It was his work apron. He was going before God with Israel on his heart and Israel on his shoulders.

In the priest's breastpiece, there were two stones he would cast as lots for right-or-left, yes-or-no decisions. They were called the Urim and the Thummim, the "lights and the excellencies." The high priest would represent the nation before God and God would give them guidance. Gideon made an ephod as if to say, "If you people are not spiritual enough to go back to worship God through the priest, then I will bring the priest to you. I will bring him out from the holy place here so you can seek God."

Is that prescribed in the Old Testament? It is not. Gideon is progressive. Like Paul warns, he "exceeds what is written" (1 Corinthians 4:6). You don't do that. You depart from the Bible by denying it, and you depart from the Bible by adding to it. Remember, the second commandment, "You shall make no graven image of God" (see Exodus 20:4). That's what we do when we try to make God approachable by coming down to man's carnality. Gideon made it into an ephod and placed it in *his* city, Ophrah. In other words, he gives it the presidential stamp.

We're seeing for the first time in a judge, theological compromise. Where do you think this text will end? We're changing who God is and we're going to change how we approach Him. "All Israel,"—what's the next three words?— "Played the harlot." They didn't fool God. This is idolatry. They played the harlot with it there and it became a snare to Gideon and his household. This theological compromise is going to bring a moral compromise. That moral compromise is going to bring a political compromise, in that a man will be put in office who had no business being there. And he's going to kill all but one of Gideon's sons.

We're about to have a bloodbath just like the pagans had. Remember this about theology, one might depart from it but they are going to have to pay the fiddler after the dance. In verse 28, Midian was subdued before the sons of Israel and they didn't lift their heads anymore. Gideon was a good military leader.

Note, it never says Gideon judged Israel. He ruled them. The other judges make moral calls. Gideon didn't. You know why? Because he compromised his Bible. Like a liberal in the pulpit, he's got nothing to say about morality having denied biblical authority. The land was undisturbed for forty years. In verse 29, "Then Jerubbaal . . ." that is Gideon's nickname. Jerubbaal means, "Let Baal contend with him." He became a marked man. "Jerubbaal the son of Joash went and lived in his own house." It's called retirement. He headed to Florida.

He lived in his own house. He doesn't just retire. You never retire as a man of God, you transition. You get the next generation ready. In verse 30, he had seventy sons. You're saying to yourself, "He wasn't *that* busy." No, I don't think so. They were his direct descendants because he had "many wives." Those two words are a first, a watershed. You've never seen it in the law of God. Why many wives? The reason he had many wives is to have many sons. The reason he wanted many sons is that even though he's not going to be a king, he can establish what is called an oligarchy. It's where you get a small group, a politburo, to govern for you. He's going to install his boys in governing the nation. His concubine in Shechem, in the tribe of Ephraim, bore him a son, and Gideon named him Abimelech, meaning "My father is king." You know what I think? I think Gideon, after ruling for a while, realized God wasn't going to rule this nation because this nation had departed.

Gideon looked at those people and said, "No, they're going to need a leader and this is a special son." He names him, "my father is the king," Abimelech. Then "Gideon the son of Joash died at a ripe old age and was buried in the tomb of his father Joash, in Ophrah of the Abiezrites. Then it came about, as soon as Gideon was dead, that the sons of Israel again played the harlot" (vv. 32–33). The theological concession didn't work.

Like a stream running beneath the bank, if you let a stream run under the riverbank long enough, what's going to happen? Overnight, it's going to come down. They played the harlot, not with merely an ephod, but with the Baals. They fell into full-blown Canaanite worship of nature and made Baal-berith their God, "Baal of the covenant."

The sons of Israel did not remember the Lord their God, the true "Lord of the covenant," who delivered them from the hands of all their enemies on every side. Israel departed from their historic roots. Israel departed from the God of the Exodus journey, the conquest of Joshua, and the God of Gideon. Is it possible for a nation to turn and bite the hand of the one who fed them? Yes, and that's what they did. They did not show kindness to the household of Jerubbaal, that is Gideon, in accord with all the good which he had done.

They forgot God, and they forgot their national heroes, the ones who stood for them historically. They turned against Moses, their historic, biblical hero who established them. How quickly can a nation do a total 180? That's what they did. In Judges 9:1, out of this spiritual theological decay, a root, a weed, jumps up. Abimelech, son of Jerubbaal, went to Shechem, to his mother's relatives, his immediate family. He spoke to them and to the whole clan of the household of his mother's father, his extended family, and said, "Speak now to the leaders of Shechem."

He starts with a small group of family members and then he goes to the local politicians. He's going to impose a certain belief on them. It's called getting a critical mass. You can't lead a revolution by yourself. Hitler had to have the Beer Hall Putsch in Munich. Lenin had to have the October Revolution. He did it in Moscow. The French revolutionaries did it in Paris. Abimelech did it in Shechem. He got a critical mass. Here was his offer, "Which is better for you, that seventy men, all the sons of Jerubbaal, rule over you, or that one man rule over you?" (v. 2).

The rule of the seventy was what Gideon tried to do. Gideon was to have an oligarchy. But Abimelech said, "Make me king." He wants absolute rule. This is Mussolini. This is Joseph Stalin. This is Fidel Castro. "I want absolute authority."

This is called absolutist rule, or fascism. A *fasci* is a term from Rome about a bundle of sticks you would beat with. Fascism is where you oppress. We have here a king? No, we have a fascist absolutist rule, and it's not going to be to seek the living God. Abimelech must get rid of God. He says in verse 2, "And also remember, I am your bone and your flesh." Meaning, "I'll make it worth your while. Don't look at my platform of what I believe. Look at me as to whether you like me. Remember, you are my family. There's something in it for you. You can get a free ride if you put me in charge."

Is there ever a possibility people can vote because of personal interest groups? It's the essence of American politics. They're completely oblivious to God, but thinking *I can get something out of this.* Abimelech's mother's relatives spoke all these words on his behalf and the hearing of the leaders of Shechem. Now his constituency manipulates local government. You have here a tension between the national government and the local government. The man at the national helm is going to manipulate those at the local level to get what he wants.

In verse 3, they were inclined to follow Abimelech because, in effect, they said, "He's our relative. He's our homeboy. There are perks for putting him in place." Next, we need to have a campaign contribution. In verse 4, they gave him seventy pieces of silver from the house of Baal-berith. We have evil money from an evil theology, with which Abimelech, an evil man, hired evil men to followed him. We are watching a tsunami begin. It's starting small but it's growing. But now, if you're going to be an absolutist rule and get rid of the earlier administration's people, what are you going to have to do to secure yourself?

Ever study history? It's what every leader does. You kill everybody who can in any way disagree with you. It says he killed his brothers, the sons of Jerubbaal—seventy men on one stone. It was a sacrifice—a sacrifice to Baal. An official act of apology for what Gideon did in his day. You may remember in the book of Judges whenever Gideon began his judgeship, he was told by God to pull down the altar of Baal in his father's backyard. Everyone said, "Who pulled down this?" They said, "Gideon did."

His father said, "If Baal is God, let Baal deal with him." They nicknamed him, "Let Baal contend with him," Jerub-Baal, God's man against Baal worship. This boy Abimelech made a national apology to the gods of the Canaanites. "I'm sorry for what we did." This is called revising history. He's going to change theology; he's going to change gods. Is he changing morality? Is he changing the dignity of man, "thou shalt not kill"? We have a theological, moral, spiritual, political collapse, and it took place overnight.

All the men of Shechem and Beth-millo made Abimelech king. We started with the immediate family, then the extended family, then the local leaders, and now the men of Shechem and the men of Beth-millo. The revolution is growing. He would have been shouting out like Elizabeth Warren, "Come, join the revolution."[4] They made Abimelech king by the oak of the pillar in Shechem.

Now, let me tell you what that means. Shechem was a holy site in Israel. Whenever Abraham came out of Ur of the Chaldees, he stopped at Shechem, Genesis 12:6. There he built an altar by the oak of Shechem. The oak of Shechem was called the oak of Moreh, "the oak of the teacher." It was where you had pagan ideals and pagan religion taught in Canaan. God made him build an altar at the oak of Shechem. It was Abraham's statement, "There is a new God in the land." It's like the Washington Monument. It's the Lincoln Memorial. It's Lexington. It's Concord. When Abraham wanted to buy land to bury Sarah on, guess where he bought land—Shechem.

This is where Machpelah is, the Tomb of the Patriarchs. This is Arlington Cemetery. Jacob in his return to Canaan stopped in Shechem, when he came out from Paddan Aram. And he had a little daughter named Dinah who was raped. Then Simeon and Levi killed every man in Shechem. Jacob said, "You have done turned the whole Canaanite people against us." He said, "Boys, y'all have been compromised. I want all your idols. I want all your earrings, give them to me" (see Genesis 34–35). He took them and he buried them. You know where he buried them? At the oak of Shechem.

Shechem is a Levitical city. Shechem is a city of refuge, a holy place. As a matter of fact, the name "Shechem" means "the shoulder." It's as if God carries you. He makes a national apology at the Lincoln Memorial and says, "We as a nation have done wrong in getting rid of idolatry." There is no opposition from the nation. Where's the nation? They're silent. Let me tell you what I learned a long time ago about bad politicians. They run under the cover of apathy.

In our church we put out voter guides for people to know who wants their hands on their children. But here the people never show up. In verse 7, there's one man, Jotham. He was the youngest child of Gideon. I love these next three words—"he went and stood." There was one lone voice from one young man. The older men didn't do anything, but the young man did.

One lone young man stood on top of Mount Gerizim. Shechem is between Mount Gerizim and Mount Ebal. The base of the mountain is 500 yards from the other one. In Deuteronomy 11, God said when you go into the land I want you to take six tribes and put them on Gerizim, six tribes and put them on Ebal.

On Gerizim, they call out the blessings. On Ebal, they call out the curses. Why do we have the law of God established on mountains? Because mountains don't move. Like the law of God. This man took his place back on a historic monument and he called out the place of blessing. It's as if he said, "You want blessing? You're not going to get it from this murderer and this idolater. You're going to get it from God."

He went and stood on top of Mount Gerizim. He lifted his voice and he called out. Circle that. "He lifted his voice." How many voices do we have? One little junior high guy. "What you're doing ain't right." He said, "Listen to me, O men of Shechem that God may listen to you." Meaning, "If you don't listen to me, you are alien from God." There was no moral confusion to this man. "Turn from me, and you turn from God. You turn from me, and God will have nothing to do with you." Does he sound a little dogmatic? Yes, he does. He put the dog in dogma.

"You turn from God, you turn from the word I'm about to enunciate, and God will have nothing to do with you." Then he said, "Once upon a time, the trees went forth to anoint a king" (v. 8). Trees being like the men of Shechem to anoint a king like Abimelech. "They said to the olive tree, 'Reign over us!'" The olive tree is a good place to go to get a king. The olive is where you get anointing oil, and it's where you get light, holiness, and truth. Incidentally, do you know what the word "anointed" is in Hebrew? Messiah. In the Greek, it's pronounced, "Christ." They went to the right tree.

A holy man and a wise man. Go to that man. Not simply a countryman who can give you gift cards. The olive tree said no. "Shall I leave my fatness with which God and men are honored and go wave over the trees?" (v. 9). You know when you wave over the trees? It's when you try to be the top tree. He said, "I have no ambitions to be numero uno. I want to have fatness to serve God and serve men. I want to bring God and men together." Now, that's what a politician is meant to be. "I am going to establish the rule of God."

The trees then went to the fig tree. Now if an olive makes you holy, a fig tree makes you healthy. They're like the dessert of Israel. "You come reign over us." The fig tree said, "Shall I leave my sweetness and my good fruit?" (v. 11). Meaning, "I want to make people healthy. I want to improve society. I don't want a place of ambition." Then the trees went to the vine, the place of happiness where you would take new wine at the feast days and celebrate the goodness of God. "You reign over us." The vine said, "Shall I leave my new wine, which cheers God and men?" (v. 13). It makes men be appreciative of what God has done. That delights God, and that delights us.

All of them want to be a blessing to God and men. Finally, the tree said to the bramble, to the thorn bush, "You come, reign over us!" (v. 14). Who do you think the thorn bush will coordinate to? Abimelech. A thorn bush is painful; it's dead, it's dry. The only thing you can do is to chop it down with a sword and burn it. Incidentally, where do thorns come from? The curse. There was a Man in the Bible who wore a crown of thorns. Yes. It's a judgment. They went to the bramble and said, "You come reign over us."

The bramble said to the trees, he speaks to the voters, to those who want to put him in power, "If in truth you're anointing me as king," meaning, "If it is from a divine motive you're looking for the blessing of God to make me king, then that's good. Come and take refuge in my shade." That's sarcasm. Ever tried to snuggle up under a bramble tree? You can't. "But if not . . ." meaning, "If you're putting me in power because of your personal interests, if you're putting me in power because there's something about my platform that makes evil easy for you, may fire come from the bramble and consume the cedars of Lebanon" (see v. 15).

Does it take a little while to grow cedars of Lebanon? Takes a lifetime. How long does it take to grow bramble? No time. Put him in power because of your sin, and fire is going to come from him. Your choice is going to come back on you. Evil men can take all that has been accomplished since 1776 and burn it to the ground overnight.

But in verse 16, he said, "Let me apply this parable. If you dealt in truth and integrity in making Abimelech king, if you voted for Abimelech because he's a holy man, a healthy man, a happy man with God. If you've dealt well with Jerubbaal, the hero who stood for you and dealt with him as he deserved for my father fought for you and risked his life. If you're in keeping with the law of God and the history of good men" (author's paraphrase).

But in verse 18, "But you have risen against my father's house today and have killed his sons, seventy men." Incidentally, who killed the seventy men? Abimelech. Who does Jotham say killed them? The voters. In effect, "You are as responsible as the evil you put in place. If you did this because he is your relative, because of personal interest, because you could get perks, or if then you've dealt in truth and integrity with Jerubbaal in his house, rejoice in Abimelech."

It's as if he said, "If you put a man in who fears God and loves his fellow man, you're about to have a great experience because the divine decision is found on the lips of a king that he should not impart an error. And let him rejoice in you because you've put a man in place that all he's going to be concerned about is your good. Rejoice in him. But if not, let fire come forth and consume you" (see vv. 19–20).

When you think of fire coming forth, what do you think of? At Sinai from the Holy of Holies and consuming Nadab and Abihu.

It's divine judgment. Put a godless politician in place simply because he strokes you where you like it and lets you do what you are pleased to do and will not stand in opposition, then your government is going to take you down. God is not going to have to judge you. Your choice is going to judge you. And it will also come from the men of Shechem and from Beth-millo and consume Abimelech. Because very soon they wanted Abimelech dead. The man they put in place here, in about thirty-six months, they will want him dead.

Benito Mussolini was killed when one of his guards shot him and his wife, and the guards hung them by their heels outside their house. The people of Italy poured out upon them and tried to rip his body to shreds because he sent the nation to its death. In the same way, men are going to hate this Abimelech.

Then Jotham fled. Because he knew when you have a godless leader, you have no freedom of speech and so he took off running. He went to Beer, and he remained there because of Abimelech, his brother.

Joseph Stalin once said death solves all problems. Hitler would send you to the chambers. Stalin would send you to a gulag. You would disappear. Stalin sent Solzhenitsyn away because Solzhenitsyn in his diary spoke of Stalin as "the man in the mustache."

The Khmer Rouge wouldn't even bother with a camp. They'd take you out and kill you. That's why, a few years back, a fellow started digging in Cambodia and turned up a bunch of skeletons. They called it the killing fields. You get a godless man—you can't stay there. "We've got to get rid of you and we've got to silence your voice," or as Mr. Rousseau said, "Some people must be forced to be free."

Verse 22, Abimelech ruled for three years. Why for three years? I think God let the people stew in their own grease. "I'm going to make you enjoy this guy because in three years you will want another revolution." Then in verse 23, a name appears that has not appeared throughout the narrative. Who's the name? God. God isn't running for God. The Bible says God will not align Himself with a throne of mischief (Psalm 94:20). You think God can be fooled? God says, "I know who you are. I've got eyes of fire." God sent an evil spirit.

God does not make good men evil, but He can make evil men more evil for His own purposes. Of Pharaoh, "For this very purpose, I raised you up to demonstrate My power in you, and that My name might be proclaimed throughout the whole earth" (Romans 9:17). God said to Satan, "Sic 'em. I'm going to take back the fence. You want to play with Satan, you got Satan."

They dealt treacherously with Abimelech. It's called poetic justice. As you did, it is done to you, "so that the violence done to the seventy sons of Jerubbaal might come, and that their blood might be laid on Abimelech their brother who killed them, and on the men of Shechem who strengthened his hands" (Judges 9:23). Meaning, "You people that voted for murder, I hold you as guilty as that man. I'm going to judge him, but I'm going to judge you *by him* for what you did."

The men of Shechem set men in ambush on tops of mountains and they robbed all who might pass by them on the road and it was told to Abimelech. Why did they do this? To draw out Abimelech. They go and rob people. I think it's because Abimelech's system of government failed. When you reject God, what will you rule by? What's your standard? You will be lenient or oppressive. You have no basis of rule. Water can't rise beyond its source, and so we'll get a godless man. The Bible says, "Where there is no vision," meaning, prophetic revelation, "the people are unrestrained" (Proverbs 29:18).

Whenever you remove God, you remove the mortar of society. So it was with Abimelech. The leaders were warned "You will not get grapes from a thorn bush."

In verse 26, here comes a *new* revolutionary—Gaal the son of Ebed came with his relatives. We've got another man with another bunch of relatives. We've just got a new bunch of revolutionaries. Nobody's seeking God. The solutions now are going to be worse than the problems.

What's this proverb mean? "By the transgressions of a land, many are its princes" (Proverbs 28:2). You keep having revolutions, and new cartels because no one wants to return to God. And so they put their trust in him, went into the field, and gathered grapes in the vineyards and trod them, and they held "a festival" (Judges 9:27). "We have new confidence and a new god." Like a political convention.

They went into the house of their god and they ate and drank and they cursed Abimelech—they had a *new* leader.

They said, "Who is Abimelech, and who is Shechem, that we should serve him? Is he not the son of Jerubbaal, and is Zebul not his lieutenant?" (v. 28). They didn't like the presidential appointee there in Shechem, so they said, "Serve the men of Hamor, the father of Shechem."

Gaal said, "My bloodline goes back not to Shechem but to Shechem's daddy, Hamor." Hamor in Hebrew means "the ass." (Be careful when you put your trust in an ass.)

He said, "Would that these people were under my authority!" We have new promises. "Then I would remove Abimelech." Really? Gaal said to Abimelech, "Increase your army and come out." What are we about to have here? It's called a civil war, and it only took thirty-six months because we had a theological, spiritual, moral collapse in religion and in politics.

We can skip ahead here to verse 44, and I'll show you how the war between Abimelech and Gaal went. In verse 44, then Abimelech and the company who was with him dashed forward and stood in the entrance of the gate. They lured Gaal out of Shechem, and then Abimelech went in behind them and cut off their retreat. They can't get back in the city. The other two companies then dashed against all who were in the field. We have them in what's called a pincer movement. Does this sound familiar? It's like the Red Sea coming down.

Then Abimelech fought against the city all that day, and he captured the city. This is Shechem. He captured the city and "killed the people." What did Jotham promise? "Fire is going to come forth from you, from this man, and consume you" (see v. 15). He killed the people who were in it then he razed the city, meaning he took it to the ground like a razor and then he sowed it with salt that it would never flourish again, and so he made Shechem an archeological dig.

Incidentally, Shechem is the city of the patriarchs. You remember in John 4, Jesus stopped in Samaria and Jacob's well was there, and He met the woman at the well? That is Shechem.

The leaders of the tower of Shechem are Abimelech's voting constituency. These are the leaders of his electoral party who put him in place. They heard of it and they entered the inner chamber of the temple of El-Berith to protect themselves from the men they put in power.

They go into the temple of a pagan called the god of the covenant. Does anyone want to speculate as to whether this faith is going to work? "It was told Abimelech that all the leaders of the tower of Shechem were gathered together" (v. 47). Now, remember what Jotham's prophecy said, "Fire is going to come forth from this godless politician and he's going to consume you because you are as guilty as him."

Abimelech went to Mount Zalmon, he and all the people who were with him, and Abimelech took an ax in his hand and cut down a branch from the trees, lifted it, and laid it on his shoulder. He said to the people who were with him, "What you have seen me do, hurry and do likewise" (v. 48). Incidentally, that is classic irony. Do you know who else in the book of Judges said, "When we come to the outskirts of the camp, look at me and do likewise"? It was Gideon. "Follow me with my pot, my lamp, and my trumpet. Follow me and do likewise" (see Judges 7:17–18).

Did the men of Gideon defeat the Midianites? Yes, overwhelmingly. And so Abimelech is quoting Gideon, maybe he can get some deity to help him. All the people cut down his branch and followed Abimelech and they put them on the inner chamber. They set the inner chamber on fire over those inside, so all the men of the tower of Shechem died—a thousand men and women.

They are burned alive. They are surrounded by fire.

I had a fireman tell me one time, I asked him, "What's it like to be in the middle of a fire?" He replied, "What you think is that it will be overwhelmingly blinding. It isn't. The fire sucks out all the light." He said, "You're in a black hole." That's hell. Abimelech brought hell on earth to a people. Isn't politics wonderful?!

"Then Abimelech went to Thebez, and he camped against Thebez and captured it" (v. 50). Why does he go to Thebez? Because Abimelech is a beast and knows no boundaries, a tyranny has begun. But there was a strong tower in the center of the city. I don't think these people had fallen into idolatry. The Bible says the name of the Lord is a strong tower and the righteous run to it and are safe. There's a strong tower in the center and all the men and the women with the leaders of the city fled there and shut themselves in. Then they went up to the roof of the tower. Abimelech came to the tower and fought against it, and approached the entrance of the tower to burn it with fire. "I'm going to do the same thing. I've got the formula." Little does this fool know the reason he won the previous battle at Shechem was because of the sovereign justice of God using him for His own purposes, to judge His people who fell away.

Abimelech approached the entrance of the tower to burn it, but a certain woman threw an upper millstone. An upper millstone is what you would turn to grind your wheat and make it into flour. This woman headed off upstairs and she just said, "I need something," and she grabbed the millstone.

She threw the upper millstone on Abimelech's head—like David's stone to the head of Goliath and the arrow to the chest of Ahab—crushing his skull. Then he called a young man, his armor bearer, and said, "Draw your sword and kill me, so that it will not be said of me, 'A woman slew him'" (v. 54). If you were about to die, what would you be concerned about? Hell. He's concerned about how he's going to look in the casket. What happened here is we had sudden judgment, unexpected, providential, and humiliating. God removed everything. God can take an evil man out anytime He wants to.

Then it says, "The young man pierced him through." He dies by his own hand. Such is evil government; it will turn on itself. Abimelech was going to have this great monarchy—he lasted thirty-six months. He didn't make it one term. "The men of Israel saw that Abimelech was dead and each departed to his home" (v. 55). They just gave up.

Thus, at the end of the narrative, who was in charge? Look at that last verse 56, who's in charge? God. "God repaid the wickedness of Abimelech, which he had done to his father in killing his seventy brothers"—and, watch this—"God returned all the wickedness of the men of Shechem on their heads." In other words, "I hold you as guilty as him because you put him in power." Who's the only one standing at the end? Jotham and the curse he uttered in verses 19–20.

First Peter 1:24–25 says, "All flesh is like grass, and all its glory like the flower of grass. The grass withers, and the flowers fall off, but the word of the Lord endures forever." The last one standing is the man of God. The curse of Jotham, son of Jerubbaal, came.

About four years ago, I did a message called "The Continental Divide" and when I finished it, I said the barbarians are at the gate. The barbarians are not at the gate any more. They're in the square. They're in places of power. This is what happens when the people of God depart from the Bible. The whole society collapses. What are the lessons here? They're simply these. First, theological moral departure will bring political disaster.

Isn't it interesting the century that has so rejected God, and looked to science and reason, is the twentieth century? We don't have religions much anymore. We have ideologies. Fascism, Communism, Nazism, existentialism. The generation of apostasy, the century of apostasy, is the century of blood. There have never been people killed like in the twentieth century. Second, a Jotham has to stand. The faithful have to get on top of a mountain. They have got to speak up.

Third, evil will punish itself. Give it time. Fourth, God will not align Himself with a throne of mischief. You may sneak into government but God knows who you are. Fifth, men are not put in power because you personally like them. They are put in power because of what they believe. Sixth, those who put evil men in power are as guilty as they are. When you go to that voting booth, you are not alone. Somebody sees you.

Don't worry about your political choice. I'll tell you what I'm going to do. If they're going to murder the unborn,

I'm not voting for them. If they are going to make sodomy a civil right, I am not voting for them.

Seventh, if you're going to turn cities into sanctuaries for lawbreakers, if you will let evil take refuge, I'm not voting for you. If you will try to combat racism by systemic racism, if you will try to combat the racism of whites toward blacks, by systemic racism of blacks toward whites, or that I'm now guilty because of my birth certificate, I'm not voting for you there. I'm not saying who I'm voting for but if I have to apologize to God for voting for a political platform, I'm not going to vote for him or her.

And that's the story of Abimelech, the man who would be king. Or perhaps we could call him the Bible's first politician. He is very important to the Bible's narrative. Let's summarize his story:

1. He was born at a time when the nation was longing for a king, for true leadership.
2. He arose at a time of theological, moral breakdown in Israel.
3. He sought the support of a personal interest group to whom he made campaign promises.
4. He found financial support from a wicked source.
5. He took over by murder and the killing of any who might oppose him.
6. He sought a cancel culture mindset. A rebellion against the nation's spiritual history.
7. His followers were soon disappointed and disgruntled.
8. And they soon sought his overthrow.

9. And they found a new evil man with new promises and a new revolt.
10. Internal war began within the factions of Abimelech and Gaal.
11. Abimelech was used to destroy those who first followed him and put him in power.
12. His greed and ambition burst forth in an attempt of national takeover.
13. This ambition led him to a humiliating death.
14. Jotham the prophet was the last man standing.
15. His warning to Shechem is a political warning to all mankind. "Unworthy leaders will destroy the country that put them there."

And such is the message from God about country.

8

Time of Our Testing

2 THESSALONIANS 2:1–10

*Now we request you, brethren, with regard
to the coming of our Lord Jesus Christ and
our gathering together to Him, that you not
be quickly shaken from your composure or be
disturbed either by a spirit or a message or a
letter as if from us, to the effect that the day
of the Lord has come. Let no one in any way
deceive you, for it will not come unless the
apostasy comes first, and the man of lawlessness
is revealed, the son of destruction, who opposes
and exalts himself above every so-called god or
object of worship, so that he takes his seat in
the temple of God, displaying himself as being
God. Do you not remember that while I was
still with you, I was telling you these things?
And you know what restrains him now, so that
in his time he will be revealed. For the mystery*

*of lawlessness is already at work; only he who
now restrains will do so until he is taken out of
the way. Then that lawless one will be revealed
whom the Lord will slay with the breath of His
mouth and bring to an end by the appearance
of His coming; that is, the one whose coming is
in accord with the activity of Satan, with all
power and signs and false wonders, and with all
the deception of wickedness for those who perish,
because they did not receive the love of the truth
so as to be saved.*

In all of Paul's letters to the churches, he always spoke to a very special problem or need the church had. And so it was for the church in Thessalonica. False teachers had been saying the tribulation had already begun and the church was going to go through the wrath of God.

They also taught that their loved ones who died would now miss the rapture when it occurred. They also taught that a Christian could quit working and mooch off the church and wait for the Second Coming. Paul answers all these eschatological errors in 1 Thessalonians.

The classic text on the rapture in chapter 4 answers the question of whether the dead will miss the rapture. "The dead in Christ shall rise first" (1 Thessalonians 4:16). He also answers the question of mooching in chapter 4. "Work with your hands . . . that you may behave properly toward outsiders and not be in any need" (vv. 11–12).

And in 2 Thessalonians 2:1–10 he answers the question of whether the church will go through the tribulation. Let's examine each phrase.

"With regard to the coming of our Lord Jesus Christ and our gathering together to Him . . ." That is talking about the rapture.

". . . that you may not be quickly shaken from your composure or be disturbed by a spirit, message, or letter as if from us that the day of the Lord has come" (v. 2). Paul is talking about a false teacher or a false letter, a lying letter, that the tribulation has started. Make a note that Paul regarded the idea of going through the tribulation as being "shaken and disturbed." No one rejoices when they are experiencing the wrath of God. We have no hymns about going through the tribulation.

Then Paul says, "it will not come unless the apostasy has come first" (v. 3). Before the tribulation begins, there will be a worldwide rejection of the gospel and of the Christian worldview. Paul said to Timothy, "In the last days difficult times will come" (2 Timothy 3:1). We have not seen a worldwide apostasy although it is drawing close.

" . . . and the man of lawlessness is revealed" (2 Thessalonians 2:3). This is the anti-Christ. We haven't seen the anti-Christ because the time of the tribulation has not come. Paul is not saying we *will* see him, only that he must come first and we have not seen him.

But there is a third thing that must occur. First apostasy. Second, anti-Christ. And third, the "restrainer" is taken away (see v. 7). Who is the restrainer? It is the Church. As Lot restrained wrath in Sodom. As Noah and the gathered restrained the flood. As Rahab and the gathered restrained the destruction of Jericho. Peter said the reason judgment has not begun is because "the patience of our God is salvation . . . not wishing for any to perish but for all to come to repentance" (2 Peter 3:15, 9). Our presence and the work we are doing restrains the final judgment of God.

"For the mystery of lawlessness is already at work . . ." (2 Thessalonians 2:7). The word "mystery" is always referring to an aspect of the Church and the age of the gospel of grace to all men. "The mystery of lawlessness" is speaking of the allowance of sin to continue because of the mystery of the Church's purpose of ingathering of the elect. Why does God allow such evil? Because He is saving a people.

". . . only he who now restrains . . ." The Church restrains God's judgment in a lawless day. Why? That's the mystery. God's salvation is at work.

". . . will do so until he is taken out of the way." Once we are removed and the sheep gathered, the judgment will begin and the anti-Christ will appear.

". . . whom the Lord will slay by the breath of His mouth and bring to an end by the appearance of His coming" (v. 8). This is the return.

Paul wrote to the Romans, "I do not want you to be uninformed of this mystery [again the mystery of the Church] . . . that a partial hardening has happened to Israel until the fullness of the Gentiles has come in; and so all Israel will be saved" (11:25–26).

"A partial hardening has happened to Israel." Israel is under a judicial darkness with "eyes to see not and ears to hear not." But it is *partial*. Not all Jews are darkened but some are being saved. And the hardening of Israel is not *final*. Someday all the nation will believe when Jesus returns and removes sinners from the nation and "all Israel shall be saved." But the hardening is very purposeful. It is "until the fullness of the Gentiles has come in." This is talking about the elect of God. Jesus said, "All the Father gives Me will come to Me, and the one who comes to Me I will certainly not cast out. . . . but [I will raise him] on the last day" (John 6:37–39).

God has a purpose in our day. A "mystery." The Church. He is gathering a people. With every day, evil is rampant. But with every day while sin is escalating, God is saving a people.

When you peruse the book of Revelation, you see in the tribulation (chapters 6–18) the word "Church" does not appear. The emphasis is on the nation of Israel. We are symbolized in the twenty-four elders in heaven in chapter 4:11. We appear again in chapter 19 when Christ returns to rule with His bride "in fine linen, bright and clean" (19:8). In between these two mentionings is the tribulation, and we are not mentioned because we are not present for the wrath of God.

Another reason we do not go through the "hour of testing which is about to come upon the whole earth" (3:10) is because our hour of testing is right now. "In the world you have tribulation" (John 16:33). Peter said, "It is time for judgment to begin with the household of God" (1 Peter 4:17). This age with its trials is the exposé of who is and who is not a Christian. Jesus said, "and when affliction or persecution arises because of the word, immediately he falls away"

(Matthew 13:21). Paul spoke of trials to the Thessalonians saying, "This is a plain indication of God's righteous judgment so that you will be considered worthy of the kingdom of God, for which you indeed are suffering" (2 Thessalonians 1:5). Our time of testing is now. Between the cross and the crown; between the first and second comings of Christ. A period where we proclaim salvation to the world. A time when we warn the world of His return and judgment. A time when we exhibit to the world what it longs for—love and unity.

So why is this the final chapter about the Bible's view of God and country? Because this is what the Church is to be in relation to its country. We are not going to establish the kingdom of God in our time. We are not attempting to somehow replace Israel and symbolically fulfill the kingdom of God. We are a royal priesthood to our culture. God enlists us to represent the coming King to a pagan world. To speak of His person. To tell of His death and resurrection. To proclaim His salvation. To warn of His return and of His judgment. Because of the Church being the "called-out ones," our lives take on an infinitely greater purpose and meaning. In every age and in every country and culture, Christians have thrived. The light of the world and the salt of the earth. A city set on a hill. A city of refuge. Those who "give a defense when called to account for the hope" that is in them. We are those who restrain the evil in our day. We are those who after Christ has entered the strong man's house and has bound the strong man is now distributing his plunder. And Jesus said, "the one who does not gather with Me scatters" (Luke 11:23). We are co-laborers with Jesus, gathering the lost from the domain of darkness and into the kingdom of God's dear Son. Though we live in this world, we are "faraway fellers" who have a higher calling than bread and clothing but rather we seek first the kingdom of God and His righteousness.

What do Daniel, Shadrach, Meshach, Abed-nego, Ezra, Esther, Nehemiah, Zerubbabel, Mordecai, and Jeremiah have in common? They were all heroes. They all exhibited great loyalty and faithfulness. And they were all men and women of the exile. Faithful in a fallen culture and in a day of evil.

Days such as ours are where heroes are born.

It is said the great existential question of the Christian is "Why has God saved me?" The answer is solely for the glory of His grace. The second great question soon follows: "Why has God left me down here?" He has left us here to gather with Him the plunder of Satan. Jesus said, "My food is to do the will of Him who sent Me" (John 4:34). As with Jesus so it is with us. Paul said to the Philippians that his heart's desire was "to depart and be with Christ, for that is very much better; yet to remain on in the flesh is more necessary for your sake. Convinced of this . . . I will remain and continue with you all for your progress and joy in the faith" (Philippians 1:23–25). He was here for the purpose of God.

This was my great struggle as a young man in the early '70's. What am I to do with my life that will truly count for something? Only the eternal would satisfy me—something that would not leave me saying "Vanity, vanity. All is vanity."

Soon after I was converted, one of my teammates asked me what happened to me. I told him the simple gospel message. After that summer when I showed up for two-a-day workouts, I met him in the lobby of the athletic dorm. As soon as I saw him I said, "You did it." And he had. He was a new creation. He has remained my best friend to this day.

Upon seeing the eternal impact, I said, "I've found it." However I made my living, I had now found my life. "For to me, to live is Christ and to die is gain" (Philippians 1:21). Normally death undoes and destroys all your life accomplished. But with Christ "to die is gain." Death is one's final victory and ultimate fulfillment.

Think of it like this. A quarterback drops back to throw a fly pattern to a fleet wide receiver aiming to score on that one bomb. But as he sets up, a linebacker blitzes on his left to thwart his plan. But just before he sacks him, the quarterback looks to his alternative receiver to save the day. A running back has slipped out in the left flat and just before all is lost, takes the "dump" from the QB and runs for a touchdown accomplishing what the play originally intended.

Such is God's victory in this age.

Christ was the quarterback. Israel was His fleet wide receiver to score and establish the kingdom of God, but Satan was the linebacker who blitzed to destroy the victory of God. But Christ, the QB, saved the day by tossing the ball to the Church, the secondary receiver, who would accomplish what Israel lost.

And that is who we are. When Satan whispers "make yourself at home," just remember you are an alien and not of this world. We've been weaned off of leeks and onions.

But Satan has a seven-fold plan for us. "The Killer D's"

1. To *deceive* us by lies and error.
2. To *disqualify* us through sin that removes our witness.
3. To *distract* us through worldly materialistic ambitions.
4. To *discourage* us through ministerial hardship.
5. To en*danger* us into fear and silence and lack of faith.
6. To *divide* us through an inability to get along with other Christians.
7. And if all fails, *death*. He longs for our destruction.

God has chosen to glorify Himself through the mouths of the weak—through infants and nursing babes to establish praise for Himself. We are His choice sling and spear in His plans between God and country.

Notes

1. Sigmund Freud, *Totem and Taboo* (1913; repr. Abingdon, UK: Routledge, 2012), 171.

2. Friedrich Wilhelm Nietzsche, *The Complete Works of Friedrich Nietzsche: Human, All-Too-Human* (New York: The MacMillan Company, 1913), 224.

3. "Should anti-LGBT churches be tax-exempt? Texas Gov. Greg Abbott blasts Beto O'Rourke for old comment," https://www.dallasnews.com/news/politics/2022/01/19/greg-abbott-blasts-beto-orourke-for-old-comment-on-tax-exemptions-for-churches-against-gay-marriage/

4. Radical Progressive senior United States senator from Massachusetts

Five-Star Reviews
for Tommy Nelson's *The Book of Romance*

John C. Reilly
The best discussion on the Song of Solomon . . .

"Tommy Nelson is perhaps the best teacher of the Word of God I know. His multiple studies on the Song of Solomon, Ecclesiastes, and other wisdom literature have given me such insight into who God is. *The Book of Romance* is a fascinating walk-through of the Song of Solomon. In the introduction Tommy states, 'Do you think God would allow men and women to marry and then toss them a grenade called intimacy and say to them, "Well, just fiddle around a little with this and you'll figure out how to work it"?' Too many times the church as a whole skirts the issue of sex and romance even though the Song of Solomon hits it head on.

"This is an amazing study that my wife and I did while we were dating, while we were engaged, and since we have been married. I have worked in youth ministry for nearly a decade and I have taught this material to youths as well. I credit my good marriage to learning the truths Tommy points out in this book.

"I HIGHLY recommend this book."

E. Kurillo
AWESOME BOOK

"I went to a Bible study class and the subject was this book in the Bible (Song of Songs).

"We watched a DVD of Tommy Nelson preaching the subject. It was so good and I saw there was a book on Amazon. I got it. The book matches the DVD. I wanted to get the DVD but it was $200.00 and the book was $10 at the time. Tommy gives great testimonies. He teaches with a way of keeping one's attention the whole time (even with reading) and he gives excellent advice.

"I recommend this book over and over and over again. It couldn't have been written better."

Funky Pete
Great, and important for today
"This book is a rare jewel, actually explaining the Song of Solomon for what it is; a romantic and erotic love story; a play between two people, explaining how to date, marry and live together in a godly way."

P. Solomon Kovacs
Every man should read this book . . .
"Excellent overview of Song of Songs and the power and beauty of the relationship between King Solomon and his beautiful, 'dark and lovely' Shulammite bride. Every man should read this book, and then re-read as many times as needed to fine-tune his relationship with his wife to realize the depth of love, sex, and intimacy that God created as a gift within the marriage relationship. This book raises the bar high for both sexual morality and our expectations for marriage, and rightly so."

P. Baugh
Life-changing!!!!!!!!
"I cannot put this book down!!!! The book is almost entirely highlighted!! I am so grateful for amazing biblical teaching and nuggets regarding Song of Solomon that I thought would be forever elusive but thanks to Pastor Nelson I am equipped with the treasure trove of lifetime wisdom for being prepared as a godly wife!!!!!"

J
A great biblical book

"A great biblical book. This pastor teaches about what the Song of Solomon is about and breaks it all down. It's an in-depth study of the book. The main crux of the book is tenderness for the bride."

Coral
Full of beneficial information

"I'm very happy I purchased and read this book. There is a lot of beneficial information for those who are single and in relationships/married. The author talks to you like you're in the room having a discussion."

iaminthevineyard
One of the best books I've ever read

"One of the best books I've ever read that clearly explains what the true distinctions are between men and women, from a biblical perspective."

Conservachick
Changed my way of thinking forever!

"This was one of the most engaging, encouraging, and comforting books I've ever read! Tommy Nelson BEAUTIFULLY describes the Song of Solomon and applies it to our lives. I recommend this book to anyone thinking of dating, courting, anyone who is married or going through a tough marriage.

"This book makes one realize how society has ruined the reputation of dating, marriage and sex. After finishing this book—which was a very quick read—I found myself completely desiring to be married in order to experience the wonderfulness Tommy Nelson's book on the Song of Solomon has shared.

"This is a MUST read!"

Unnamed buyer

A wise book

"I generally refrained from reading the Song of Solomon because I didn't understand it—until now.

"Tommy Nelson uses his keen wit and delight in biblical history to explain the Bible's most frequently misunderstood book—the Song of Solomon.

"This is one of the most prized books in my evergrowing collection.

"If you are looking at understanding what the world's wisest man has to say about Love, Sex and Intimacy and how it can/should be applied to your relationship or marriage today—don't hesitate to purchase this.

"It took me awhile to pick up the book because I thought it would be a dry 'thou shalt not' book—it's completely the opposite. It talks about 'thou shall' especially if you are married.

"If I knew it was going to be this good, I would have read it five years ago."

Brian Reaves

Truly an amazing and deep book!

"I recently read through Song of Solomon truly paying attention for the first time. It was an incredibly romantic and poetic read. Then I found this book and read through it, only to find that I had missed SO MUCH in Song of Solomon and the meaning behind what was said! This book is amazing, and Tommy Nelson teaches it in plain English and doesn't resort to 'preacherspeak' so many other authors go for. This would make an excellent Bible study for any singles group interested in talking about proper dating, courtship, marriage, and beyond. This is, by far, the best Christian book I've read in a long time."